元宇宙的元理论研究

Metatheory Study
of the Metaverse

清华大学马克思主义学院 中国移动咪咕公司 著

华文出版社
SINO-CULTURE PRESS

图书在版编目（CIP）数据

元宇宙的元理论研究：汉文、英文／清华大学马克思主义学院，中国移动咪咕公司著. —— 北京：华文出版社，2023.4（2023.5 重印）
ISBN 978-7-5075-5807-4

Ⅰ. ①元… Ⅱ. ①清… ②中… Ⅲ. ①信息经济－汉、英 Ⅳ. ①F49

中国国家版本馆CIP数据核字（2023）第062391号

元宇宙的元理论研究
Metatheory Study of the Metaverse

作　者：	清华大学马克思主义学院　中国移动咪咕公司
执 笔 人：	孙洁民
策划编辑：	杨艳丽
责任编辑：	袁　博
营销编辑：	张　露　赵小峦
出版发行：	华文出版社
地　　址：	北京市西城区广安门外大街 305 号 8 区 2 号楼
邮政编码：	100055
网　　址：	http://www.hwcbs.cn
电　　话：	总编室 010-58336210　编辑部 010-58336191
	发行部 010-58336267　010-58336202
经　　销：	新华书店
印　　刷：	北京博海升彩色印刷有限公司
开　　本：	880mm×1230mm　1/32
印　　张：	6.625
字　　数：	120 千字
版　　次：	2023 年 4 月第 1 版
印　　次：	2023 年 5 月第 2 次印刷
标准书号：	ISBN 978-7-5075-5807-4
定　　价：	59.00 元

版权所有，侵权必究

本书编委会成员

朱安东　（清华大学）　　刘　昕　（中国移动咪咕公司）

何建宇　（清华大学）　　王　刚　（中国移动咪咕公司）

孙洁民　（清华大学）　　冯　林　（中国移动咪咕公司）

Members of the Editorial Board

Tsinghua University: Zhu Andong, He Jianyu, Sun Jiemin

Migu Culture Technology Limited Company: Liu Xin, Wang Gang, Feng Lin

《元宇宙的元理论研究》课题组主要成员

朱安东　（清华大学）　　刘　昕　（中国移动咪咕公司）

何建宇　（清华大学）　　王　刚　（中国移动咪咕公司）

孙洁民　（清华大学）　　冯　林　（中国移动咪咕公司）

李秋甫　（清华大学）　　王寒英　（中国移动咪咕公司）

孔奕淳　（清华大学）　　朱　泓　（中国移动咪咕公司）

欧阳兰榛（清华大学）　　徐浩华　（中国移动咪咕公司）

吕俊彦　（清华大学）　　曹慧华　（中国移动眯咕公司）

乔成治　（清华大学）

黄怡暄　（清华大学）

Main Members of the "Metatheory Study of the Metaverse" Research Group

Tsinghua University: Zhu Andong, He Jianyu, Sun Jiemin, Li Qiufu, Kong Yichun, Ouyang Lanzhen, Lü Junyan, Qiao Chengzhi, Huang Yixuan

Migu Culture Technology Limited Company: Liu Xin, Wang Gang, Feng Lin, Wang Hanying, Zhu Hong, Xu Haohua, Cao Huihua

序言（一）

进入 21 世纪以来，全球科技创新空前活跃，以移动通信、人工智能、物联网、量子信息、区块链为代表的新一代信息技术加速突破，正在重构全球创新版图、重塑全球经济结构。2022 年 11 月 9 日，习近平总书记在致 2022 年世界互联网大会乌镇峰会的贺信中指出，当今时代，数字技术作为世界科技革命和产业变革的先导力量，日益融入经济社会发展各领域全过程，深刻改变着生产方式、生活方式和社会治理方式。元宇宙作为信息技术革命的一种未来图景，既是我国国有企业大有可为的广阔蓝海，又是创新发展马克思主义的宝贵机遇。

马克思主义是一门与不断变化的条件相适应的历史科学，必须随现实条件的变化而发展。日新月异的科学技术和经济生产是马克思主义的沃土。面对新现象新问题,不应寄希望于从本本中找到现成答案,更不应照搬照抄西方理论。坚持马克思主义的科学方法论,立足实践建构中国自主的知识体系,是马克思主义守正创新之道。我们与中国移动咪咕公司筹建联合研究中心并展开合作研究,正是为了更好地立足中国大地,讲好中国故事,发展中国理论,服务中国实践。

马克思主义是科学的理论,是人民的理论,是实践的理论,是不断发展的开放的理论。深化马克思主义研究,推进中国式现代化在理论和实践上的创新突破,离不开对生动的中国实践的参与和体悟。清华大学马克思主义学院与中国移动咪咕公司联合展开的关于元宇宙相关基础理论的前沿研究,是坚持马克思主义基本原理与中国具体实际相结合,不断推进马克思主义中国化时代化的有益尝试。在研究过程中,双方研究人员充分发挥各自优势,多次展开集中研讨,反复打磨书稿内容,在对马克思主义的理解运用和对信息技术及其产业发展的认识把握上都取得长足进步,实现了 1+1>2 的协同效应,探索出一条校企合作的新路子。

　　元宇宙是新生事物，本身就处于迅速发展变化的过程中。对元宇宙的超前研究具有战略意义，但由于时间和水平所限，难免存在疏漏甚至错误之处，欢迎广大读者特别是学界业界同行提出宝贵的批评、意见和建议。

朱安东
2022 年 11 月 9 日于清华园

序言（二）

当前，人类社会正加速步入信息文明时代，信息和能量作为驱动人类文明进步的两条主线，正由相对独立发展向彼此融合创新演变。作为数字经济的代表性产业和全新赛道，"元宇宙"连续数年成为行业热词，并成为数字经济的战略前沿。

中国移动立足创世界一流"力量大厦"战略和"一二二五"战略实施思路，发力元宇宙等前沿领域。中国移动咪咕公司较早开展了元宇宙的实践探索和路径研究，并致力于产学研深度融合，提高科技成果转化和产业化水平。

为进一步探索元宇宙建设和文明，2022年，中国移动咪咕公司与清华大学马克思主义学院联合筹建"智慧党建与思政联合研究中心"，并发布《元宇宙的元理论研究》,旨在探索关于元宇宙的世界观、方法论、价值观及相应话语体系等根本理论问题,并在马克思主义大的理论体系下,构建关于元宇宙的"中国自主的知识体系"。

在追求全人类共同价值、构建人类命运共同体的时代背景下,"元宇宙应该是什么",这是一个具有战略性和全局性意义的重要理论问题。联合研究中心的建立,就是要发挥元宇宙最大的价值,使其成为实现全人类共同价值的数字时空和推动构建人类命运共同体的重要方式。

探索中国式元宇宙创新模式,对于推动千行百业数字化转型、满足人民的美好生活需要具有重要意义。中国移动咪咕公司将充分发挥5G+算力网络优势,沿着"元宇宙的MIGU演进路线图",通过"内容+科技+融合创新",携手各方伙伴共同打造中国特色元宇宙新生态,助力网络强国、数字中国、智慧社会建设,为全球产业发展贡献中国标准、中国方案、中国力量。

正值春暖花开、万物生长之际,为读者奉上这本关于元宇宙基础理论之作,希望能为探索元宇宙的未

来提供一份参考。由于时间有限，加之研究也是一个不断演进的过程，本书难免有不尽全面和疏漏之处，请方家批评指正。

是为序。

刘　昕

2023年4月

目 录

引言　为元宇宙文明贡献中国之智　　　　　　　1

一　元宇宙研究概论　　　　　　　　　　　　　5
　　1.1 元宇宙学及其元理论　　　　　　　　　5
　　1.2 元宇宙概念　　　　　　　　　　　　　8
　　1.3 元宇宙文明　　　　　　　　　　　　　9
　　1.4 元宇宙建设与元宇宙治理　　　　　　　12
　　1.5 元宇宙的元理论研究　　　　　　　　　15

二　时空建构：来自科学技术史的启示　　　　　18
　　2.1 作为人造物质系统的元宇宙　　　　　　19
　　2.2 标识能量利用水平的元宇宙　　　　　　21
　　2.3 标识信息传递水平的元宇宙　　　　　　23

三　工业革命：来自经济基础的推动力　　　　　27
　　3.1 工业革命的一般规律　　　　　　　　　28

3.2 元宇宙适应第四次工业革命需要 　　　　　30

3.3 元宇宙必然推动经济基础的变革 　　　　　33

3.4 从"工具机革命"看元宇宙前景 　　　　　38

四　价值哲学：追求自由而全面的发展　　　42

4.1 元宇宙体现人类对自由而全面发展的追求　　43

4.2 元宇宙价值规范性问题的战略性和全局性　　45

4.3 元宇宙是科技革命对人类共同命运的回答　　47

五　文明有序：元宇宙治理的中国方案　　　50

5.1 建设元宇宙文明的治理挑战 　　　　　　　51

5.2 以文明有序的元宇宙走向元宇宙命运共同体　54

5.3 新时代元宇宙治理的政策原则 　　　　　　58

5.4 构建元宇宙文明生态系统 　　　　　　　　62

六　结语　　　　　　　　　　　　　　　　64

6.1 如何理解元宇宙概念 　　　　　　　　　　64

6.2 携手迈向元宇宙文明 　　　　　　　　　　66

参考文献　　　　　　　　　　　　　　　　68

Preface (I)   73

Preface (II)   77

Introduction: Contributing Chinese Wisdom to the Metaverse Civilization   81

Chapter 1   Metaverse Research Overview   87

Chapter 2   Spatiotemporal Construction:

Insights from the History of Science and Technology   106

Chapter 3   Industrial Revolution:

A Driving Force from the Economic Foundation   118

Chapter 4   Value Philosophy:

Pursuing Free and Comprehensive Development   140

Chapter 5   Civilized and Orderly:

China's Solution for Metaverse Governance   151

Chapter 6   Conclusion   173

Endnotes   180

References   189

引言　为元宇宙文明贡献中国之智

我们是新一轮科技革命的亲历者和见证人。2021年5月28日，习近平总书记在中国科学院第二十次院士大会、中国工程院第十五次院士大会和中国科学技术协会第十次全国代表大会上的讲话中指出，当前，"科技创新速度显著加快，以信息技术、人工智能为代表的新兴科技快速发展，大大拓展了时间、空间和人们认知范围，人类正在进入一个'人机物'三元融合的万物智能互联时代"①。这是党中央对我们当前面临的新一轮科技革命大势的基本判断。

新一轮科技革命必将推动人类社会的系统性变革。量子科技、大数据、云计算、扩展现实、人工智能等前沿科技日新月异的进步使人与自然的关系、人与社会的关系乃至人与自身的关系的发展接近从量变到质变的临界点。科技进步在给人类带来空前丰裕和效率的同时，也伴生经济、伦理、情感、安全等方面的风险和隐患；不仅如此，资本主义制度的固有矛盾使18

---

① 《习近平谈治国理政》第4卷，北京：外文出版社，2022年，第196—197页。

世纪下半叶以来生产力革命的成果从未让全人类共享。能否变革不公正不合理的全球治理体系，使新一轮科技革命的成果充分惠及全人类，是亟待国际社会解决的重大问题。对此，中国有责任也有能力贡献中国智慧和中国力量。2022年11月9日，习近平总书记向2022年世界互联网大会乌镇峰会致贺信指出："当今时代，数字技术作为世界科技革命和产业变革的先导力量，日益融入经济社会发展各领域全过程，深刻改变着生产方式、生活方式和社会治理方式。面对数字化带来的机遇和挑战，国际社会应加强对话交流、深化务实合作，携手构建更加公平合理、开放包容、安全稳定、富有生机活力的网络空间。……中国愿同世界各国一道，携手走出一条数字资源共建共享、数字经济活力迸发、数字治理精准高效、数字文化繁荣发展、数字安全保障有力、数字合作互利共赢的全球数字发展道路，加快构建网络空间命运共同体，为世界和平发展和人类文明进步贡献智慧和力量。"这是在新一轮科技革命及其引发的广泛社会变革背景下，对"人类向何处去"这一重大问题给出的中国答案。

党的二十大报告提出加快建设网络强国和数字中国，将新一代信息技术和人工智能等定位为新的增长引擎，指出要加快发展数字经济，促进数字经济和实体经济深度融合，打造具有国际竞争力的数字产业集群。这是在中国式现代化这个总课题下，对数字经济的战略定位。

元宇宙作为信息技术革命的未来图景，是网络强国和数字中国拼图的重要板块，也必然是实现中国式现代化，推动构建人类命运共同体，创造人类文明新形态的物质基础。然而，对于元宇宙这一新趋势新现象，包括中国在内的广大发展中国家远未发挥科技和理念上的引领作用。这意味着，当前在网络空间全球治理中存在的不公正不合理现象乃至霸权霸凌霸道行径，有可能衍生至元宇宙全球治理中。

解释元宇宙的话语权、建设元宇宙的主导权、治理元宇宙的议题设置权和规则制定权，应当且必须掌握在中国人自己手中。这就要求我们积极展开前瞻性探索。当前正逢百年未有之大变局，如何在实现中国式现代化和构建人类命运共同体的高度上认识元宇宙，中国能否在元宇宙这片新天地提出并探索出一条导向人类命运共同体的解决方案，是本书的研究背景和核心关怀。

为元宇宙发展发出中国声音、提供中国方案，需要科学理论的支撑。习近平总书记指出，"加快构建中国特色哲学社会科学，归根结底是建构中国自主的知识体系"。本研究的核心目的就是探索关于元宇宙的"中国自主的知识体系"，具体说

来，就是建构关于元宇宙的世界观、方法论、价值观和相应的话语体系，为我国及广大发展中国家在元宇宙的全球治理中争取话语权、主导权、议题设置权和规则制定权做理论探索。

一　元宇宙研究概论

当我们谈论元宇宙时，我们究竟在谈论什么？这是研究元宇宙首先需要明晰的问题。国内外不论是舆论界还是学术界，都有观点认为元宇宙只是为商业炒作而制造的噱头。2022年11月ChatGPT发布以来，更有不少观察家断言元宇宙不过是已经过气的风口。元宇宙风头正盛则捧为掌上明珠，热度一降则弃之如敝履——这显然不是科学的态度。对元宇宙建立严肃的认知，是探索关于元宇宙的"中国自主的知识体系"的基础工作。

1.1 元宇宙学及其元理论

探索关于元宇宙的"中国自主的知识体系"，其实就是探索中国自主的元宇宙学。这要求我们思考以下几个问题：

第一，什么是元宇宙学；

第二，元宇宙学的研究对象是什么；

第三，元宇宙学的边界在哪里，也就是研究范围；

第四,我们如何研究元宇宙,也就是研究方法。

元宇宙学就是关于元宇宙的各种学说或各种理论。这是人们用头脑对元宇宙的各种具体现象进行抽象思维的产物。近几年产生的大量关于元宇宙的论文和专著,就是元宇宙学的文献。

元宇宙学的研究对象,是作为客观存在或客观趋势的元宇宙,也就是元宇宙的各种表现、现象,以及各种现象的客观演化趋势,如算力网络的进步、人工智能的进步、数字货币的推广、数智竞技的发展等。

元宇宙学的研究范围有多大,取决于研究对象所涉及的领域有多少。元宇宙学是一片涵盖自然科学和哲学社会科学众多知识领域的理论蓝海。

元宇宙学的研究方法不能一概而论。一般而言,研究方法包括两个层次,一是抽象层次上的方法论,也就是关于如何认识和研究元宇宙的总的思想原则;二是各种具体的研究方法,如案例研究法、比较研究法等。前者是后者的指导,后者是前者的表现。

不同学科领域下的元宇宙学研究,因具体的研究对象有别,具体的研究方法自然不同。但对于中国自主的元宇宙学来说,方法论应当是统一的,那就是辩证唯物主义和历史唯物主义。2018 年 4 月,习近平总书记在十九届中央政治局第五次集体学习时指出,"马克思主义理论的科学性和革命性源于辩证唯物主义和历史唯物主义的科学世界观和方法论,为我们认识世界、改造世界提供了强大思想武器",并强调要"聚焦我国改革开放和社会主义现代化建设面临的重大现实问题"。研究元宇宙,肯定要考察科学技术发展规律,这就需要辩证唯物主义的指导;元宇宙及其治理也涉及社会历史规律——比如经济规律、社会治理规律——这就需要历史唯物主义的指导。

以上内容——包括研究对象、研究范围、研究方法等——构成了元宇宙学的基本问题。对这些问题的回答方式,决定了对元宇宙的某项研究会形成怎样的具体观点。这些基本问题的总和,构成元宇宙学的元理论。"元理论"不是"元宇宙的理论",而是指关于某种理论的理论,是用以描述某个学科的基础理论的术语。

元宇宙、元宇宙学、元宇宙学的元理论,是从具体到抽象、从客观实在到理论思维的三个层次。其中,元宇宙是元宇宙学的研究对象,元宇宙学又是元宇宙学的元理论的研究对象。对作为客观趋势的元宇宙进行的各种理论研究的总和,形成元宇宙学;对元宇宙学的基本问题的理论抽象,进一步形成元宇宙学的元理论。

1.2 元宇宙概念

探索中国自主的元宇宙学,必须建立对元宇宙概念的自主理解。认识元宇宙,必须透过表象看本质。有观点认为元宇宙不过是资本为投机而炒作的概念;还有观点认为元宇宙是数字资本主义通过制造概念来回避困境的策略。基于辩证唯物主义和历史唯物主义的方法论,考察元宇宙概念归根结底是要看这一概念是否反映科学技术进步和经济社会发展的客观趋势。

着眼于科学性和严谨性,当前还没必要为元宇宙下过于精确的定义,因为成熟的元宇宙的具体形态,取决于未来相当长一段时间的科技进步和经济社会发展。我们只需要把握元宇宙的基本性质和基本趋势。这是一种科学的态度。科学理论当然具有预测的功能,但是预测必须把握尺度。

从上述原则出发,本书从三个角度定义元宇宙:

第一,元宇宙是技术聚合体、产业聚合体和生态聚合体。也就是说,元宇宙是众多技术、产业和生态聚合形成的复杂系统,其背后是实在的技术集群、产业集群和用户需求。

第二,元宇宙是信息技术革命的愿景聚合。元宇宙概念引发全球关注,根本上是因为,以往在信息技术领域,移动通信技术、云计算技术、虚拟现实技术、区块链技术等虽然会描述各自的未来图景，但都只着眼于信息技术革命的某一个分支。元宇宙概念成功为人们描绘出完整的信息技术革命愿景，使各种已有技术和技术方向在未来社会拼图中的角色和定位骤然清晰。

第三，元宇宙是"人机物"三元融合的万物智能互联的系统。从"人机物"三元融合的角度来看，可以把元宇宙概念的核心理解为时空建构。时间和空间是人类实践活动的基本维度。信息技术的发展使人类具备日益强大的时空建构能力，可以通过数字孪生等技术建构复刻现实世界（物理时空）的数字世界（数字时空）。但是，数字时空在虚拟和现实之间还存在清晰界限，没有相对独立的时间，无法提供全感官体验，只是物理时空的补充、延伸和附属。随着信息技术进步特别是人工智能向脑智能、认知智能的发展，元宇宙有望实现全感官体验，还会拥有完整的、具备再生产活动的经济系统和社会系统。如果这些得到实现，元宇宙将以现实的而不是虚拟的面貌呈现在人面前，成为可以与物理时空交融的数字时空。元宇宙的本质就是建构原生于物理时空且与之交融的数字时空。

1.3 元宇宙文明

文明是"人类在认识和改造世界的活动中所创造的物质

的、制度的和精神的成果的总和",是"社会历史进步和人类开化状态的基本标志"。① 从静态来看,文明是人类社会创造的一切进步成果;从动态来看,文明是人类社会的演化过程。②

元宇宙发展必然孕育元宇宙文明。元宇宙代表实在的技术集群、产业集群和用户需求,因此其发展必然推动人类社会的演化。在这个演化过程中,人类创造出的各种进步成果的总和,就是元宇宙文明。

人类文明诞生至今,相继演化出原始文明、农业文明和工业文明。20世纪四五十年代以来,信息与通信技术的发展推动人类社会迈向信息文明。习近平总书记指出:"从社会发展史看,人类经历了农业革命、工业革命,正在经历信息革命。"③ 这正是从社会史和文明史的角度理解科技进步的革命性作用。基于历史唯物主义,生产力与生产关系的矛盾运动构成文明演化的基本动力,文化、哲学、法律、政治和国家等的形态与形式,归根结底取决于生产力水平(技术水平):"手推磨产生的是封建主的社会,蒸汽磨产生的是工业资本家的社会。"④

---

① 《中国大百科全书》第23卷,北京:中国大百科全书出版社,2009年,第296页。
② 张瑜、闫聚群:《"网络文明"的概念辨析》,《青海社会科学》2014年第6期。
③ 习近平:《在网络安全和信息化工作座谈会上的讲话》,北京:人民出版社,2016年,第2页。
④ 《马克思恩格斯文集》第1卷,北京:人民出版社,2009年,第602页。

元宇宙文明是信息文明的高级阶段。从宏观历史尺度来看，现代人类尚处于信息文明初级阶段，即网络文明。网络文明的成果在经济上表现为生产方式和协作形态进步、交往方式丰富和交往范围扩大等，在政治上表现为行政效率提高、社会参与扩大、电子政务普及等，在文化上表现为知识传播扩大、文化创新发展、精神生活内容丰富等。① 信息技术的持续突破与融合发展将使人类真正进入"人机物"三元融合的万物智能互联时代，人类在时空建构能力的基础上形成物理时空与数字时空相交融的文明形式，从而使信息文明从初级阶段演化至高级阶段，即元宇宙文明。

数字时空和物理时空相交融是元宇宙文明的标识。在元宇宙文明之前，数字时空虽然可以在一定场景下被建构出来，但还不发达。农业文明和工业文明中根本谈不上数字时空。网络文明中虽然存在利用信息技术搭建的数字时空，但虚实之间有清晰界限，且数字时空在功能上和逻辑上都只是物理时空的补充、延伸和附属。因此，在元宇宙文明到来之前，物理时空都是人类文明绝对意义上的中心，网络空间的绝大多数活动和现象都围绕人们在物理时空中的活动而展开。元宇宙文明则不同，它使人类文明的中心从物理时空拓展到数字时空；或者说，

---

① 张瑜、闫聚群:《"网络文明"的概念辨析》,《青海社会科学》2014年第6期。

人类文明将获得物理时空与数字时空相交融的形式。

1.4 元宇宙建设与元宇宙治理

走向元宇宙文明，必须统筹元宇宙建设与元宇宙治理。

从系统论的角度考虑，元宇宙建设包括核心系统、交互系统和价值系统。

第一，核心系统，包括基础设施和支撑元宇宙的子系统。基础设施由算力网络和数字引擎构成。算力网络是以 5G 为代表的多项创新技术的融合，包括 5G、人工智能、区块链、云、大数据、网络、边缘计算、终端和安全等各项底层技术，其目标是实现网络无所不达、算力无所不在、智能无所不及。数字引擎是产业数智升级的核心驱动，推动各领域数智化转型。依托各项底层技术，形成支撑元宇宙的子系统，包括时空建构系统（算力体系、泛在智能等）、规则建构系统（信用体系、数字产权、文明生态等）和应用安全系统（数据安全、隐私安全等）等。

第二，交互系统，即在基础设施支持下，将元宇宙具象化且使之与人交互的媒介、场景和内容。媒介、场景和内容是交互系统三要素。元宇宙的各种终端和应用平台都属于媒介，不同的终端和应用平台会形成面向不同需求的元宇宙场景，不同元宇宙场景呈现不同的内容。媒介决定数实融合的逻辑和形式，也即决定人们在物理时空和数字时空之间的穿梭方式[①]，决定人们在元宇宙中的活动方式，决定场景建构和内容呈现。概言之，元宇宙中所有实践活动都是在与媒介、场景和内容的交互中实现的。

第三，价值系统，包含两个方面。一方面是人们建设元宇宙和发展元宇宙文明所秉持的价值观，这会直接影响元宇宙的规则建构系统和应用安全系统，并对交互系统建设发挥重要作用。这就意味着必须审慎思考：我们期待的元宇宙是什么样的？是一个有助于实现人的自由而全面发展的元宇宙，还是一个充满剥削、欺诈、暴力和安全隐患的元宇宙？另一方面是元宇宙中所有活动所必然包含的价值观念。人们在元宇宙中的所有实践活动都会在其自身和元宇宙留下烙印，这些烙印既会塑造其自身的价值观念，又会影响他人的价值观念。价值观念不是先天的或凝固不变的，而是在人的实践活动中形成并且被不断塑造的，既会被自己影响，也会被他人和环境影响。在这个

[①] 所谓穿梭，是指人们可以随时随地接入和退出元宇宙，也就是在物理时空和数字时空之间实现无缝切换。当交互系统可以支持数实穿梭，才意味着"人机物"三元融合得以实现，元宇宙才达到发达水平。

意义上,"媒介即是讯息。"①,而讯息即是观念——媒介、场景和内容既受价值观影响,也会塑造价值观;既会影响活动者的价值观,也会影响他人的价值观。因此,元宇宙建设必须首先回答元宇宙向何处去、服务于谁的问题。

对上述三个系统的区分意味着元宇宙的底层逻辑是技术与价值规范的复合物。目前,元宇宙尚在孕育,技术路径不一,前景远未明朗,必定会在国际市场上经历长期的积累、试错和竞争。元宇宙的未来直接取决于市场竞争,而什么样的元宇宙产品能够赢得市场竞争,又取决于它的基础设施是否足够完善、交互系统是否足够发达及价值系统是否凝聚人心。

作为典型的信息技术应用,元宇宙必然存在网络效应。网络效应是指产品满足用户需求的程度与产品中社会网络的规模相关,用户数量越多,每个用户能从社会网络中获得越大的价值。搭建元宇宙应用场景,制定元宇宙治理规则,倡导元宇宙文明生态,归根结底要解决用户来不来、认不认的问题。没有足够庞大的用户基础,就谈不上话语权、主导权、议题设置权和规则制定权。反过来,企业为了在市场竞争中吸引用户,可能会默许甚至迎合猎奇、低俗、色情、暴力等内容的存在。所

---

① [加]马歇尔·麦克卢汉:《理解媒介——论人的延伸》,何道宽译,北京:商务印书馆,2000年,第33页。

以，建设元宇宙，有效的引导和规范不可或缺，否则就容易出现资本无序扩张。

因此，元宇宙的价值系统居于统揽全局的地位。如果在价值系统上失去元宇宙建设的主导地位，那么即便在核心系统和交互系统有所建树，也难以确保产业安全和意识形态安全，更难以满足习近平总书记关于科技创新三个"共同"的要求[①]。

1.5 元宇宙的元理论研究

越是可能产生革命性影响的新技术新产业，越不能采取跟跑战略，越需要独立自主，因而越需要前瞻性的理论探索、战略布局和科学引导。

元宇宙文明能否满足全世界人民对美好生活的向往，不是纯粹的技术问题或经济问题，还关乎伦理道德、国家治理、国际竞争等上层建筑因素，以及科技创新、能源供给等经济基础因素，是高度复杂的系统问题。构建人类命运共同体，实现全人类共同价值，是元宇宙文明题中应有之义。习近平总书记在中共中央政治局第三十九次集体学习时强调："弘扬中华文明

---

① 2021年9月24日，习近平总书记向2021中关村论坛视频致贺时强调："通过科技创新共同探索解决重要全球性问题的途径和方法，共同应对时代挑战，共同促进人类和平与发展的崇高事业。"

蕴含的全人类共同价值，推动构建人类命运共同体。"让元宇宙文明为每个人自由而全面发展开辟道路，中华文明理应有所作为。

习近平总书记强调："坚持和发展中国特色社会主义，必须高度重视理论的作用。"[①] 时不我待，引领元宇宙文明，在理论研究上要抓住"牛鼻子"，从根本上解剖元宇宙。唯有如此，才有可能充分认识元宇宙的顶层设计，才有可能充分认识元宇宙蕴藏的机遇和潜在的挑战。因此，本书直接下沉到元理论层次，尝试为中国自主的元宇宙学及面向人类命运共同体的元宇宙发展确定坐标。

本书并不是一般地讨论元宇宙学的基本问题和基础理论，而是尝试在基本问题和基础理论的层次上建构关于元宇宙的"中国自主的知识体系"，因此本书以"元宇宙的元理论研究"为题。在这一主题下，本书主要从历史必然性、客观现实性、价值规范性和治理公共性等四个方面考察元宇宙：

以辩证唯物主义和历史唯物主义为方法论，本研究首先要考察元宇宙概念究竟是营销话术，还是反映实在的客观趋势。这就是研究元宇宙的历史必然性和客观现实性，研究元宇宙从哪里来、为何而来，对应本书的第二章和第三章。

---

① 《习近平谈治国理政》第 2 卷，北京：外文出版社，2017 年，第 62 页。

元宇宙的发展不是纯粹的技术问题。任何技术应用于社会，都会衍生出伦理、规范和治理问题。在本体论意义上，元宇宙是人类实践的创造物：先有的人类社会，才有的元宇宙。这意味着什么呢？一方面，元宇宙不可能凭空发展，必须与现实社会相协调。这不是只靠元宇宙产业内部就能解决的问题，必须依赖国家战略、产业政策和基础设施投资等支持。另一方面，如果发展元宇宙反而干扰和破坏经济社会发展和文明进步，那就本末倒置、舍本逐末了。所以对元宇宙不能自由放任，必须重视价值观和治理观问题。这就要研究元宇宙的价值规范性和治理公共性，也就是回答元宇宙向何处去、服务于谁，对应本书的第四章和第五章。

二 时空建构:来自科学技术史的启示

如何界定元宇宙?基于辩证唯物主义和历史唯物主义,要回答这一问题,就要考察元宇宙概念是否反映某种客观存在或客观趋势,也就是从科学技术进步和经济社会发展的客观规律来认识元宇宙。

元宇宙概念虽源自科幻小说,且目前主要是对现有技术的集成,但其代表的技术体系、技术范式和技术创新趋势却是实在的。元宇宙的必然性和现实性植根于科学技术进步的客观规律中。因此,元宇宙并不是虚妄的概念。反过来说,如果不坚持从科学技术进步的客观规律出发去认识和界定元宇宙,那么对元宇宙的理解就容易滑向幻想。

物质、能量和信息是自然界的基本要素。从人与自然的关系来看,科学技术史就是人类日益认识物质、能量和信息并加以开发利用的历史。基于物质、能量和信息这三个维度,可以考察元宇宙的历史必然性和客观现实性。

2.1 作为人造物质系统的元宇宙

辩证唯物主义认为，系统是自然界及其中一切物质的存在形式。贝塔朗菲将系统定义为"相互关联的元素的集"[①]，钱学森将系统定义为"由相互制约的各个部分组织成的具有一定功能的整体"[②]。

根据某个系统相对于人类社会是否具有先在性，可以区分出自然系统和人造系统。天体、海洋、生态系统等都属于自然系统。人造系统存在于自然系统中，是人类实践的产物。手机、互联网、城市等都属于人造系统。如果关于元宇宙的设想成为现实，那么元宇宙显然也是人造系统。

系统不仅是物质存在形式，还会发生演化。在没有外部指令干预的情况下，系统由内部各元素或子系统的相互作用而自发形成有序结构的演化过程，就是自组织。[③]激光、细胞、生态系统、人类社会、地球都属于自组织系统。

开放是系统演化的前提。开放系统在其边界与环境发生物

[①]〔奥〕L.贝塔兰菲：《一般系统论：基础·发展·应用》，秋同、袁嘉新译，北京：社会科学文献出版社，1987年，第46页。
[②] 钱学森、宋健：《工程控制论》上册，北京：科学出版社，2011年，第X页。
[③]〔德〕H.哈肯：《信息与自组织：复杂系统的宏观方法》，郭治安译，成都：四川教育出版社，1988年，第29页。

质和能量交换。只有当开放系统与外界的物质和能量交换驱动系统远离平衡态,负熵流大于熵增,系统才有可能向耗散结构转化,孕育新结构,实现演化。①正如理论物理学家普里戈金所言:"非平衡是有序之源。"②

人类社会发展是典型的开放系统自组织。实践是人类社会与自然界实现物质和能量交换的过程,是推动作为开放系统的人类社会远离平衡态的不竭动力。在所有实践形式中,科学技术的推动力最为强大——马克思认为,科学是"一个伟大的历史杠杆"③,是最高意义上的革命力量。

移动通信、扩展现实、人工智能、大数据、数字引擎等信息技术的发展已经使"人机物"三元融合的人造物质系统成为可预测的趋势。当前的网络空间还只是物理时空的补充、延伸和附属,不可能脱离来自物理时空的指令而存在。元宇宙在"人机物"三元融合的基础上实现数字时空与物理时空的交融;由此,人的意志就不再是来自系统外部的指令,而是系统内部的元素。在这个意义上,元宇宙也可以被理解为从数

---

① 段晓君、林益、赵城利编著:《系统科学教程》,北京:科学出版社,2019年,第121—122页;吴国林主编《自然辩证法概论》,北京:清华大学出版社,2018年,第39—40页。

② Ilya Prigogine, "Time, Structure and Fluctuations," *Science*, 1978, vol.201, no.4358, pp. 777-785.

③ 《马克思恩格斯全集》第25卷,北京:人民出版社,2001年,第592页。

字时空—物理时空交融的角度描述未来人类社会运行特征的概念。

2.2 标识能量利用水平的元宇宙

能量就是物理系统做功的本领。能量是人类实现生存并进行所有实践活动之所必需。只有首先获取并利用能量，才能改造环境、生产产品、传递信息、建立组织。在运用能量的基础上，人类得以从事日益发达的生产活动，进而支撑起日益丰富的社会生活和日益发达的文明形态。

能量来自对能源的开发和利用。能源是可以直接或经转换提供能量的载能体资源，是人类文明的物质基础。当代人类社会运转所需要的几乎一切能源本质上都是太阳能。新石器时代的农业革命使生物质能成为人类文明史上最早开发利用的能源。18世纪中叶开始的工业革命以蒸汽动力的大规模应用为核心，人类进入蒸汽时代。19世纪60年代的第二次工业革命使人类进入电气时代。电力成为新型动力，使大量生产和大量消费成为现实，资本主义生产的社会化大大增强。不仅如此，当代人类以电力为基础的丰富物质生活，正始于这次革命。因此，第二次工业革命也称电力革命。20世纪四五十年代开始的第三次工业革命，使人类的能量利用水平再次增强。从核能到各种清洁能源的开发，使电力获得更广泛更充足的能量基础。以电力为前提，计算机技术和信息通信技术才获得广阔天地，并让人类建立网络空间。

人类文明的重大进步都伴随着能量利用水平的提高。一方面，当能量利用水平迈上新台阶，人类就有条件获得新的动力形式，以此开发和驱动新的生产资料；另一方面，人类社会生产生活日益增长的需要必然推动能量利用水平进步。[①]

从能量利用水平的发展规律看，元宇宙已初步具备客观现实性：其一，能量密度不断上升、能源品质从高碳向低碳发展是世界能源发展总趋势。[②] 当前，清洁能源开发正在取得突破，可控核聚变有望实现既无穷无尽又清洁环保的能源供给。2020年，新一代可控核聚变研究装置"中国环流器二号M"建成并成功放电。一旦人类掌握可控核聚变技术，就可以使"人造太阳"梦想成真，支撑起元宇宙建设必然消耗的巨大电力。其二，在清洁、稳定、不竭的能源供应基础上，算力才有可能稳定地驱动元宇宙。风帆、风车等属于风力机械系统，水磨、水

---

① 邹才能、赵群、张国生等：《能源革命：从化石能源到新能源》，《天然气工业》2016年第1期。

② 邹才能、何东博、贾成业等：《世界能源转型内涵、路径及其对碳中和的意义》，《石油学报》2021年第2期。

轮机等属于水力机械系统，蒸汽机、内燃机等则属于热力机械系统。元宇宙是人类在数字时空与物理时空交融基础上建立的物质系统，其动力由算力系统支持，算力则依靠物理时空的电力保障。因此，元宇宙将是新一轮科技革命在能量利用水平上取得突破后结出的果实。

当然，实现元宇宙所需要的能量利用水平依然面临严峻挑战。[①] 尽管"新能源革命"正加速到来，但第二次工业革命以来，人类对能量的开发利用尚未出现堪比蒸汽机和电力那样的颠覆性进步。高度发达的能量利用水平是元宇宙的绝对物质前提，要实现类似《雪崩》《头号玩家》等科幻小说和科幻电影的元宇宙体验，既需要能源技术革命，也需要硬件和软件协同推动算力革命，以更低的能耗支持更强大的算力，应对数据密度和数据总量激增带来的挑战。

2.3 标识信息传递水平的元宇宙

信息反映系统要素之间的关联方式。信息不是物质，但其存在必须依托介质或载体；信息本身没有能量，但信息传递需

---

① 王轶辰：《元宇宙能过"能源关"吗》，《经济日报》2022年1月27日第6版。

要能量。从信息论的角度看，信息是对不确定性的消除。① 从声音到文字，从科学技术到文化艺术，从协作到国家治理，无不需要信息。

物质系统从简单到复杂的演化，是熵减和信息增加的过程。越发达的物质生产、越先进的科学技术、越远距离的通信和协作、越高级的社会形态，意味着越发达的信息传递水平。

电报技术→电话技术→广播电视技术→有线互联网技术的发展史，是人类社会信息传递水平单向一对一→双向一对一→单向一对多→双向有线多对多的进步史。20世纪80年代至今，移动通信技术实现从1G到5G、从模拟语音到趋向万物智联的突破，实现双向无线多对多的信息传递。信息传递密度的跃升使媒介体验实现移动通话→短信→网络视频→短视频的升级。信息传递能耗的下降使信息处理能力剧增，在过去半个多世纪中，计算机处理器在性能提升上亿倍的同时，耗电量下降90%。②

信息传递水平的进步史就是信息媒介和媒介体验的进步史，它有六大维度：其一，及时，解决信息时效性随信息传递时间的增加而降低的问题；其二，方向，与及时同样重要，生

---

① Claude Elwood Shannon, "A Mathematical Theory of Communication," *The Bell System Technical Journal,* vol.27, no.3, 1948, pp. 379-423.

② 吴军:《全球科技通史》，北京：中信出版社，2019年，第363页。

产协作和日常生活的需要推动媒介从单向到双向再到多向，方向越多则效率越高；其三，感知，人们日益可以调动更丰富的感官来传递和接收信息，这同时意味着信息媒介的集成程度提高，可以支持多重感知；其四，便捷，信息媒介的便捷性是信息传递效率的重要保证，媒介越便捷，越容易实现及时的通信，越能降低使用者的负担；其五，能动，在技术加持下，用户在信息传递体系下发挥主观能动性的空间日益增大，使信息的呈现方式更加多元，呈现内容更加丰富；其六，能耗，传递等量信息的单位能耗趋向降低。

目前，人类已经接近万物可数、万物皆媒的历史节点。元宇宙概念描绘的信息技术革命远景恰恰是信息传递水平在及时、方向、感知、便捷、能动和能耗这六大维度上进一步变革的可能：其一，致力于在算力网络和数字引擎等的支持下实现实时反馈；其二，致力于在高水平互操作性基础上实现万物互联；其三，致力于实现高临场感和高沉浸感，实现全感官体验；其四，致力于实现以丰富的终端形式随时随地穿梭于物理时空和数字时空，实现便捷穿梭；其五，充分释放人的能动性，解放创造力，使用户人人成为元宇宙内容的生产者；其六，致力于实现强大算力的同时显著降低单位能耗，走绿色低碳循环的元宇宙发展之路。

只有实现实时反馈和万物互联,才能创造全感官体验。人类对现实的认识和把握首先依托于感性经验,因此全感官体验甚至已超越虚拟现实,成为数字时空、数字现实。数字现实将把人们带入全新的实践场域,从而为创造力解放开辟道路。

三 工业革命：来自经济基础的推动力

科学技术水平是元宇宙的硬性条件。科幻小说和科幻电影对元宇宙的想象，也只有当相关技术在理论或实践上显露可能性时才会出现。不过，科学技术并非独立演化，其根本推动力源于社会需要，特别是经济基础中的需要。

元宇宙的生命力根源于现代生产方式发展的客观需要。物质生产对社会历史发展具有根本决定作用，生产方式在整个社会生活中居于支配性地位。"每一历史时代主要的经济生产方式和交换方式以及必然由此产生的社会结构，是该时代政治的和精神的历史所赖以确立的基础，并且只有从这一基础出发，这一历史才能得到说明。"①

基于历史唯物主义的方法论，考察元宇宙的经济必然性，根本上是要考察元宇宙能否满足经济发展的某种客观需要，或者说推动经济基础演化的矛盾是否可能催生元宇宙。解释经济基础演化，归根结底要考察生产力和生产方式。迄今为止，物

---

① 《马克思恩格斯文集》第 2 卷，北京：人民出版社，2009 年，第 14 页。

质生产都是人类社会存在和发展的绝对前提，生产力是历史发展的根本决定力量。因此，本章首先考察工业革命的一般规律；然后基于新一轮工业革命的客观趋势，在物质生产领域分析元宇宙的经济必然性；随后将视角从物质生产领域扩展到整个经济基础；最后，本研究结合工业革命史，尝试回答元宇宙的大发展还需要满足哪些客观条件。

3.1 工业革命的一般规律

工业革命是经济史学术语。尽管工业技术变革是工业革命的基础和重要特征，但工业革命概念远不限于"工业的革命"，而是涵盖一定时期内技术、经济、社会和文化的广泛转型和变革。18世纪60年代以来，人类社会已经历过三次工业革命，当前正经历第四次工业革命。

自第一次工业革命以来，物质生活的生产方式经历了手工生产→标准化生产→模块化生产→智能化生产的演化历程。生产方式以生产力为基础，而生产力水平直观地反映在生产资料水平上。生产力发展及其推动的生产方式演化，使企业从早期的同地异步协作发展为当代的异地即时协作。当前，企业网络是最发达最具代表性的协作方式。推动生产方式演化的动力是什么呢？从生产力的角度看，是科学技术进步。推动历次工业革命的科技进步都是由关键科技创新引发的连锁革命，其中能源技术和通信技术具有执牛耳的作用：前者意味着能量利用水平的提升，后者意味着信息传递水平的提升。人类据此可以开发和建立新的物质系统，直接改变协作的形式和规模，推动生产工具、交通工具和通信方式的革新。正如杰里米·里夫金所言，工业革命主要是通信方式和能源体系的变革。①

推动科技进步的根本动力又是什么呢？是社会需要。恩格斯指出："社会一旦有技术上的需要，这种需要就会比十所大学更能把科学推向前进。"②资本主义生产方式产生后，占有剩余价值的需要促使资本占有、利用并投资发展科学技术。马克思说："资本不创造科学，但是它为了生产过程的需要，利用科学，占有科学。"③在社会主义制度下，发展科学技术的社会需要不再被资本增殖裹挟，而是转变为解放和发展生产力，满足人民对美好生活向往的需要；因此，社会主义国家的政府和国有企业不仅注重推动科技进步，更注重让科技进步和生产力发展的成果为人民所共享。

---

① Jeremy Rifkin, *The Empathic Civilization: The Race to Global Consciousness in a World in Crisis*, Penguin, 2009.
②《马克思恩格斯文集》第10卷，北京：人民出版社，2009年，第668页。
③《马克思恩格斯全集》第37卷，北京：人民出版社，2019年，第203页。

如前文所述，元宇宙的发展还需要能量利用水平和信息传递水平的进一步革命，这又为第四次工业革命注入强劲动力。

3.2 元宇宙适应第四次工业革命需要

2008年国际金融危机以来，世界经济仍未走出停滞泥潭，发达国家不约而同地将摆脱困境的希望寄托于实体经济。"再工业化""工业4.0""未来工业战略"等成为美国、德国、日本等发达国家的战略布局。受新冠肺炎疫情和国际政治经济局势影响，我国经济增速放缓，制造业面临从开拓增量市场到升级存量市场转变的挑战。利用工业元宇宙突破存量市场内卷困境，有望为中国制造向中国智造的转型升级助力。在这一背景下，工业作为整个物质生产领域的核心，呼唤工业元宇宙的出场。工业元宇宙是工业数字化转型和工业互联网的未来形态。[①]

对于第四次工业革命来说，先进制造的社会需要突出表现为以下几重矛盾：第一，需求与设计的矛盾。由于存在信息不对称和信息传递迟滞，企业对需求的感知还不够敏捷。第二，需求与成本的矛盾。在模块化和智能化生产基础上，小批量、

---

① 孙柏林：《工业元宇宙——现实世界与虚拟世界互通的桥梁》，《计算机仿真》2022年第7期。

多品种和快速迭代的个性化定制成为主流,但机器设备和生产线布置、维护伴随的固定资产投资成为资本循环的制约。这导致企业即便可以及时感知需求,也需要克服成本问题。第三,设计与制造的矛盾。复杂工业品,特别是功能复杂、应用标准高的工业品,其研发、测试、认证流程复杂,在从设计向制造的转化过程中不可避免地伴随相应的高成本与高风险。

矛盾是推动事物发展的力量。在物质生产领域,尤其是在工业生产中长期的迭代式技术进步,已经使信息物理系统、三维设计、扩展现实、数字孪生、人工智能、物联网、云计算等技术形成体系,融汇成工业元宇宙的图景。工业元宇宙既是对以上几重矛盾的响应,也将革新生产方式,促进社会生产力的解放和发展。马克思指出:"社会的生产力是用固定资本来衡量的,它以物的形式存在于固定资本中。"[1]因此,生产力进步将直接反映在构成工业元宇宙的物质资料中,表现为覆盖产品设计、工艺开发、试产测试、产线生产、设备调试、产线巡检、远程维运、经营管理、人员培训、市场营销等工业生产全过程的智能系统。[2]

工业元宇宙的发展将成为应对上述几重矛盾的利器:

---

[1]《马克思恩格斯全集》第31卷,北京:人民出版社,1998年,第93页。
[2] 闫同柱:《工业元宇宙就是下一张全真工业互联网》,《中国经贸导刊》2022年第6期。

其一，强化反馈。在企业与用户之间建立实时反馈的沟通场景，增强企业对用户需求的感知能力，有效化解信息不对称和信息传递迟滞问题。企业还可以让用户在数字时空中预先体验和测试产品，根据用户反馈改进产品研发。

其二，降低成本。利用数字孪生等技术对生产布局、工艺、物流、供应链、安全保障和设备维护等进行仿真模拟，在实际配置产能和人员动线前进行验证，提高生产规划效率，减少资源消耗，降低维护成本，助力生产安全。[①]

其三，提高效率。工业元宇宙可以帮助全球生产网络中身处不同国家和地区的企业、开发者和用户在数字空间中形成高效协作，从而克服地理阻隔对协作效率的负面影响。工业元宇宙可以对产品研发全过程进行高精度仿真和模拟，在数字环境中展开试验验证和产品性能测试，提高测试效率，降低测试环节伴生的成本。

工业元宇宙是20世纪60年代以来工业数字化、信息化、智能化和服务化经长期技术积累和产业演化所呈现的技术趋势。在这个意义上，元宇宙代表实在的技术路径和经济大势。

---

① 刘大同、郭凯、王本宽等：《数字孪生技术综述与展望》，《仪器仪表学报》2018年第11期。Enis Karaarslan & Mohammed Babiker, "Digital Twin Security Threats and Countermeasures: An Introduction," 2021 International Conference on Information Security and Cryptology (ISCTURKEY), IEEE, 2021.

3.3 元宇宙必然推动经济基础的变革

第四次工业革命的发展不仅会通过工业元宇宙重塑工业，还会重塑整个经济基础，从底层的物质生产领域一直到金融系统。这种经济基础变革是必然趋势：其一，物质生产领域的变革必然推动生产关系和交换关系的变革，进而推动经济基础演化；其二，生产的发展在满足需求的同时，也不断创造新需求，新需求又反过来刺激生产发展，进而推动经济基础演化。从技术趋势和经济趋势来看，元宇宙对经济基础的系统性变革将实现生产力随算力网络分布和社会生产总过程数字化，形成经济系统的经济规律，开拓经济发展新时空。

3.3.1 生产力随算力网络分布

数字经济时代，算力就是生产力。新一轮科技革命和以智能化为核心特征的第四次工业革命正在推动人类进入万物智联时代。一方面，传统的数据中心—终端的两级模式难以满足物联网、车联网、工业互联网等特定应用场景对数据中心网络吞吐量、并发计算和存储的需求；另一方面，5G等新技术的发展使网络边缘形成海量数据，从而推动算力从少数数据中心向应用侧扩散。①同时，智能化又赋予应用侧的终端机器以更多的功能、更高的效率和更快的响应速度。这就使算力成为数字经济时代生产力的核心技术构成——算力网络覆盖到哪里，协作就可以扩张到哪里，企业就可以在多大范围内优化要素配置。

算力网络将改变生产力的分布格局，催生去中心化的生产，达到"算力所及，即可生产"的境界。对于大多数资本密集型产业（比如，冶金工业、石油工业和机械制造业）和技术密集型产业（比如，机床工业和机器人工业）来说，技术特点决定了中心化的生产不易被替代，但算力网络可以使其更加灵活和敏捷。还有一些商品和服务的生产相对更容易（比如，通过3D打印来制造），那么算力网络就有可能支撑这些产品的去中心化生产：研发设计环节依托算力网络实现自助化智能化，制造环节则可以像ATM机一样分布，甚至走入寻常百姓家。对基于比特流的数字产品来说，算力网络可以实现即时设计、即时生产、即时交付。

3.3.2 社会生产总过程数字化

社会生产总过程包含生产、消费、分配、交换（流通）四

---

① 任晓旭、谭靖超、邓辉等：《基于端边云超融合的算力网络架构》，《计算机应用》2022年第S1期；吕廷杰、刘峰：《数字经济背景下的算力网络研究》，《北京交通大学学报（社会科学版）》2021年第1期。

个环节。这四个环节并不是四个彼此独立的领域，而是有机统一于社会生产总过程中的。各种产业和业态依托于社会生产总过程的不同环节而存在和发展。

作为技术聚合体、产业聚合体和生态聚合体，元宇宙的发展必定带动大量新兴产业并在现有产业中促成新业态，实现社会生产总过程的数字化。

社会生产总过程数字化的深化会加强生产—消费—分配—交换的一体化。比如，生产力随算力网络的分散和下沉可以使生产端更敏锐地感知数字产品在消费和流通中反馈的信息，也可以使普通消费者主动借助算力网络组织个性化产品的生产，实现即时设计—即时生产—即时交付—即时消费—即时反馈。

社会生产总过程数字化必然推动数字货币和数字资产的发展，进而促成新的生产方式和商业模式。目前，基于区块链的货币转型已经成为不可逆转的趋势。以分布式账本为基础建立多中心架构的主权区块链[①]，发展主权数字货币，将成为元宇宙经济系统的血液。人们在元宇宙中依靠才智和创意创造的数字产品，一旦生成就能获得独一无二的数字权证，具有资产属

---

① 高奇琦：《主权区块链与全球区块链研究》，《世界经济与政治》2020年第10期。

性^①，其生产和流通可以带来经济价值，对用户形成激励并构成元宇宙经济系统的增长动力。在区块链技术基础上，分布式数字身份可以统合不同元宇宙细分应用场景中的数字化身，结合身份溯源就可以保护现实创作者的知识产权，并形成基于数字资产的商业模式。数字资产和现实资产的双向流通还会形成新的货币流通机制和新型商业模式。

3.3.3 新经济系统和经济规律

元宇宙经济系统以区块链技术为基础，相比互联网 TCP/IP 协议，在底层协议上实现技术跃迁：一方面，互联网底层协议不能有效保证信息安全，需要防火墙等安全保护；另一方面，互联网基于简单的底层协议和丰富的应用层协议来运作，对应用开发商的技术要求高，只有大资本才有能力开发平台级产品，普通人只能成为应用产品的使用者，在技术逻辑上必然催生平台寡头及其对数据和隐私的垄断。[②] 区块链技术降低了普通人参与的门槛，有潜力成为助力化解平台垄断和数据垄断的力量。

元宇宙经济系统必定形成新的经济规律和经济制度。经济

---

① 司晓：《区块链数字资产物权论》，《探索与争鸣》2021 年第 12 期。
② 袁园、杨永忠：《走向元宇宙：一种新型数字经济的机理与逻辑》，《深圳大学学报（人文社会科学版）》2022 年第 1 期。

规律都是历史的，经济制度都是生成的。其一，当人类以数字身份接入后，其数字生产和数字消费不仅可以（在一定程度上）脱离现实生产，而且必然形成与现实生产不同的规律，推动经济制度演化。其二，数字孪生、扩展现实等技术将提高协作效率，促进协作和生产组织形式的扁平化。区块链等技术则可能在底层逻辑上推动生产组织形式演化。其三，元宇宙中的经济活动建立在信息高效传输的基础上，可以实现生产即分发、生产即销售和生产即分配。其四，在机器人大量替代劳动力的趋势下，元宇宙经济系统可以创造新的工作和新的社会角色。如果能够有效治理垄断、建立新型分配制度，有望使人们在摆脱繁重劳动的同时，以更自由的创造活动实现经济发展和人的解放的统一，为人的自由全面发展开辟道路。

3.3.4 开拓经济发展的新时空

时间压缩和空间拓展是经济发展的两个基本维度。时间压缩主要通过生产力发展和生产关系变革，以增强协作效率、改进劳动工具、加快信息传递、改进劳动对象（比如，科学育种）等为手段实现。空间拓展一方面通过地理扩张实现，比如殖民扩张、商品输出、资本输出、海洋经济、航空经济和空天经济；另一方面通过改造既有空间实现，比如对城市地上地下

空间的重构、对城市景观的打造等。

元宇宙可以为经济发展带来更强的时间压缩和空间拓展。其一，元宇宙可以创设异地同步协作场景，大大提高全球生产网络的协作效率。其二，人可以在不同元宇宙应用场景中建立统一的数字身份，多个数字人可以在各自的元宇宙时空平行活动，形成时间倍增效应。其三，元宇宙具体应用场景中的"物理规则"与物理现实中的物理规则不同。数字现实中的"物理规则"可以被定义，而物理现实中的物理规则只能被发现和遵守，因此元宇宙中的时空不仅理论上无限，且可以一定程度上超脱于现实世界中的物理规则，使人的想象力和创造力在元宇宙中尽情释放。

3.4 从"工具机革命"看元宇宙前景

为什么元宇宙看起来前景美好，但目前还未出现具有颠覆意义的元宇宙产品？当前我们还处于以元宇宙为代表的新一轮科技革命的初期，要充分刺激和释放元宇宙蕴藏的科技革命能量，还需要寻找元宇宙的"工具机革命"。正如赵星等所说，当前仍处于"前元宇宙时代"，技术路径不一，应用场景稀缺，治理路径不明。①

马克思认为,第一次工业革命的起点不是动力革命(瓦特改进蒸汽机)而是工具机革命(珍妮纺纱机):"所有发达的机器都由三个本质上不同的部分组成:发动机、传动机构、工具机或工作机。……工具机是18世纪工业革命的起点。"②17世纪末就已发明的蒸汽机并未引起工业革命,因为直接作用于劳动对象的是工匠的手脚,而"人能够同时使用的工具的数量,受到人天生的生产工具的数量,即他自己身体的器官数量的限制"③。换言之,17世纪末的动力进步还缺乏能够充分释放其能量的应用场景,被手工生产中工匠的生理条件约束了上限。

发明珍妮纺纱机的目的正是克服手工劳动所受的生理限制。可以自动工作的工具机一旦诞生,生产力内部的矛盾就发生转化:动力供给的对象从人转变为机器,动力供给必须适应纺纱机械的高速划一运动,而人力、畜力、水力、风力都无法满足这一需要。新诞生的工具机与旧式蒸汽机的矛盾促使瓦特

---

① 赵星、乔利利、叶鹰:《元宇宙研究与应用综述》,《信息资源管理学报》2022年第4期。
② 《马克思恩格斯文集》第5卷,北京:人民出版社,2009年,第429页。马克思的理论基于19世纪的机械科学。现代机械一般分为动力系统、传动系统、执行系统和控制系统,其中前三者分别对应马克思所说的"发动机、传动机构、工具机或工作机"。在现代机械科学中,工具机一般指机床。特此说明。
③ 《马克思恩格斯文集》第5卷,北京:人民出版社,2009年,第430页。

发明双向式蒸汽机。①马克思指出："只有在劳动对象顺次通过一系列互相连结的不同的阶段过程，而这些过程是由一系列各不相同而又互为补充的工具机来完成的地方，真正的机器体系才代替了各个独立的机器。"②经济学家罗斯托指出，工业革命使"英国的发明者和革新者终于解决了用棉线作经线的问题，从而以机器同印度人的灵巧的双手展开了竞争"③。利用自然能量驱动的机器体系对体力劳动的替代，促成了农业社会向工业社会的历史性转变。④

工具机革命和动力革命构成第一次工业革命的双足，这一史实表明：动力革命及其革命能量的释放，有赖于应用场景的现实需要。

如上一章所述，算力是驱动元宇宙的动力。这个动力系统包括云计算、边缘计算、终端计算、空间计算等形态。目前，足以支持元宇宙成熟形态的算力还有很长的路要走，且需克服摩尔定律放缓的硬约束。更重要的是，元宇宙各细分应用场景尚在酝酿。面向企业用户的工业元宇宙等不乏来自细分应用

---

① 《马克思恩格斯文集》第 5 卷，北京：人民出版社，2009 年，第 432—434 页。
② 《马克思恩格斯文集》第 5 卷，北京：人民出版社，2009 年，第 436 页。
③ ［美］W. W. 罗斯托：《这一切是怎么开始的——现代经济的起源》，黄其祥、纪坚博译，北京：商务印书馆，1997 年，第 106 页。
④ 贾根良：《第三次工业革命与工业智能化》，《中国社会科学》2016 年第 6 期。

场景的需求，但面向普通消费者的元宇宙还缺少具有颠覆意义的、足以改变人们生活方式和交往方式的产品。可以想见，当前的算力系统水平可能类似于17世纪末的蒸汽动力系统。一方面需要元宇宙各种细分应用场景中的"工具机革命"，只有这些"工具机革命"在市场竞争和用户选择中彰显出优越性，才会充分激发动力革命（算力革命）；另一方面还需要工业生产（特别是芯片生产）本身的进步，从硬件和软件上支持算力技术的突破。

四 价值哲学：追求自由而全面的发展

元宇宙的价值规范性回答元宇宙"应该是什么"的价值判断问题。科学技术的进步和社会经济的发展应当推动人类的解放，而不应成为统治人的工具；应当促进社会文明水平的提升，而不应滋生社会弊病。当前国内企业界和理论界对元宇宙的理解主要着眼于"器物"，也就是从技术构成、技术趋势或经济特点来界定或解释元宇宙。[①] 任何技术都应特定的需求和目的而生，因此对元宇宙的理解决不能只有"是什么"的事实判断，更要有关于"应该是什么"的价值判断。换言之，在人类命运共同体尚未实现的大背景下，元宇宙"应该是什么"是更具战略性和全局性的维度。

---

① John D.N. Dionisio, William G. Burns III & Richard Gilbert, "3D Virtual Worlds and the Metaverse: Current Status and Future Possibilities," *ACM Computing Surveys* (CSUR), 2013, vol.45, no.3, pp. 1-38. John Herrman & Kellen Browning, "Are We in the Metaverse Yet?" *The New York Times*, Jul 10, 2021. Barry Collins, "The Metaverse: How to Build a Massive Virtual World," *Forbes*, https://www.forbes.com/, Sep 25, 2021. Kim Jooyoung, "Advertising in the Metaverse: Research Agenda," *Journal of Interactive Advertising*, 2021, vol.21, no.3, pp. 141—144.

4.1 元宇宙体现人类对自由而全面发展的追求

元宇宙是人类文明新场域,是人类通向自由而全面发展的里程碑。物理时空中的自然人在元宇宙中数字化为数字人。数字人成为元宇宙文明中的活动主体。从元宇宙文明及元宇宙社会的角度来看,数字人同时也是元宇宙中的数字公民。

从人类生命来看,挣脱自然界物理规律和生理条件的固有限制的原始冲动是人类文明演化的"基因"。从人类文明来看,文明演化的螺旋上升进程总是不断实现人更高程度的自由和解放。

人类生命的伟大就在于打破自然界中固有的"不可能",通过实践形成人化自然,强化和拓展自身的能力。早期人类文明对石器的使用,就包含着利用工具拓展头脑手脚的无限可能。船舶和潜艇使人突破水对人体的限制,飞机和飞艇使人突破飞翔的限制,书信、电报、广播、有线电话、电视、无线电话和互联网使人突破信息传递的时空限制。美国政治家汉密尔顿曾说:"机器的使用,在国家总产业中具有极为重要的作用。它是一种用以支援人的自然力的人造力量,对劳动的一切目的来说，它是四肢的延伸，是力量的增强。"①

元宇宙可以实现感知能力的飞跃。通过便捷终端接入元宇宙，人类不仅可以获得更强大的视觉、听觉、触觉等，还可以通过脑机接口、眼球追踪等技术前所未有地为感知系统赋予主动输出的能力。换言之，元宇宙可以实现感知即行动、输入即输出。

元宇宙可以实现生命形式的质变。元宇宙的意义远不止于像一般的工具和机器那样替代和延伸人的头脑和手脚，更在于以硅基赋能碳基，使碳基生命可以进入硅基数字时空。当元宇宙覆盖社会生产生活各方面，以硅材料为核心的终端设备和接口将成为人们生活之必需，甚至成为人体的一部分。碳基硅基相融合的生命存在形式是信息社会中生命形式的演化方向。

元宇宙可以助力生命的时空遍历。人的本体可以投射到多个元宇宙应用场景，以数字分身拓展实践能力和实践边界。在每一个应用场景中，都可以经历独特的时空体验。这相当于极大延长了人类寿命。工业革命以来经济系统的发展和社会文明的进步，很大程度上正是来自人均寿命的提高。有更高的寿命，人们才能更好地学习知识、生产知识并实现知识的代际

---

① Alexander Hamilton. "Report on the Subject of Manufactures (1791)," Frank W. Taussig, ed. , *State Papers and Speeches on the Tariff*, Cambridge, MA: Harvard University, 1892, p.17.

传递。

元宇宙可以重塑生活方式、交往方式和社会关系。元宇宙对人类生命的拓展必定塑造全新的生活方式和交往方式，数字身份基础上的数字生活和数字交往将形成前所未见的社会生活图景，进而反过来改变物理现实中的人。马克思指出，人的本质是"一切社会关系的总和"①。当传统的面对面交往演化出网络交往，进而在未来形成数字人在数字现实中的交往时，不仅人在元宇宙中必然形成有别于物理现实中的社会关系，而且还会反过来塑造物理现实中人的社会交往和社会关系，进而改变人本身的思想观念和行为。

4.2 元宇宙价值规范性问题的战略性和全局性

自由而全面的发展不会在元宇宙中自然而然地得到实现，这正是提出价值规范性这一元理论问题的原因。

第一，从技术进步规律来看，技术进步路径并不是唯一的或既定的，市场竞争、政府干预、资本垄断、国家竞争等多种因素都会影响技术路径。这意味着我们必须提前思考元宇宙的价值维度，以全人类共同价值引领元宇宙技术体系的演化，避

---

① 《马克思恩格斯文集》第 1 卷，北京：人民出版社，2009 年，第 501 页。

免元宇宙沦为科技巨头谋求市场份额或垄断利润的手段。以下是可能影响元宇宙技术路径的重要因素：

（1）用户需求的复杂性。如果技术创新无视伦理价值而片面满足用户的畸形需求甚至极端需求，可能导致元宇宙文明向混乱、失序的方向发展，甚至成为假恶丑的避难所和滋生地。

（2）用户沉迷的可能性。元宇宙是让人增强自身的能力以更好地认识和改变世界，还是通过沉浸而沉迷于数字时空？如果技术路径竞争得不到来自伦理价值的引领，那么必然有企业试图将元宇宙潜在的沉迷性发挥到极致来俘获用户。

（3）技术创新的目的性。技术创新主体的目的是技术路径的重要决定因素。元宇宙是要成为被少数大公司垄断以获取垄断利润的工具，或是成为被个别国家控制以实现霸权的工具，还是应当造福全社会、造福全人类？不同的目的必然刺激技术体系沿不同方向演化。

第二，社会存在决定社会意识，实践活动决定思想观念。人们在元宇宙中的活动、人们对元宇宙的体验必然改变人本身的观念和认知，如果元宇宙没有伦理道德和法律秩序的规制，很有可能使用户在其中迷失自我，甚至倒向色情、暴力和极端主义。

第三，元宇宙可以建立与物理现实交织的多个数字现实，不仅可以实现实时反馈和沉浸体验，人的本体还可以投射到数字现实中并作为数字人展开活动。这就意味着物理现实中存在的伦理道德法律问题在元宇宙中必然也存在，如不加以规制，元宇宙发展必定滋生大量相关问题乃至暴力冲突。

第四，从历史经验来看，不论是传统媒体还是互联网，都是西方国家推行话语霸权和文化霸权的阵地，占世界人口绝大多数的广大发展中国家反而没有主导权，甚至因为没有能力主导舆论而遭渗透乃至被策动"颜色革命"。因此，建设元宇宙的数字时空必须坚持文明有序的元宇宙治理观，坚持以全人类共同价值为根本关怀。

第五，从现实来看，谷歌、苹果等国外巨型垄断企业早已开始布局元宇宙并展开竞争，巨型垄断企业的背后还有西方国家政府的支持。如果在技术标准、底层协议和基本秩序的搭建上失去主导权和影响力，必然导致包括我国在内的广大发展中国家在元宇宙中继续处于话语、舆论和文化上的被动地位。

4.3 元宇宙是科技革命对人类共同命运的回答

元宇宙的价值维度在根本上回答元宇宙服务谁的问题。元宇宙应当服务于全人类共同价值而不是少数科技巨头的利润；

元宇宙应当服务于和谐的社会文明生态而不是片面迎合欲望的无度释放；元宇宙应当服务于向星辰大海的征途而不是被当作遮蔽社会矛盾的面纱；元宇宙应当服务于世界各国互利共赢而不是成为少数国家运作霸权的空间。既往历次科技革命为解放发展生产力、改变人类生活方式、拓展人类生存空间、促进政治文明和社会文明进步等方面构筑了物质基础，然而也伴生殖民、剥削、垄断、战争、金融掠夺、社会撕裂、政治极化、文化侵略、生态灾难等问题。这些问题持续困扰人类社会，有的甚至愈演愈烈。描绘新一轮科技革命远景的元宇宙，是否应该在缓解乃至解决上述问题并避免新弊病方面有所作为呢？答案显然是肯定的。

元宇宙应该是迈向人类命运共同体的阶梯和实现全人类共同价值的数字时空。积极引导元宇宙服务于全人类共同价值，应当坚持网络空间命运共同体所包含的关于发展、安全、治理、普惠等方面的理念主张[①]，走和谐、创新、绿色、安全、共赢的产业发展之路。

和谐。元宇宙中应当形成平等的社交关系、良好的文明生态和有序的数字空间。元宇宙是高阶人类文明的场域，而不是

---

① 中华人民共和国国务院新闻办公室：《携手构建网络空间命运共同体》，中国政府网，2022年11月7日，http://www.gov.cn/zhengce/2022-11/07/content_5725117.htm。

冲突、暴力、犯罪的场所。

创新。创新是元宇宙经济活动的主题,是元宇宙促成人的自由全面发展的体现。人们在元宇宙中创造的数字内容是元宇宙的活力之源。

绿色。元宇宙文明的发展离不开外部环境特别是生态环境的支撑。元宇宙的发展应坚持绿色低碳循环,在核心系统建设和交互系统建设上实现全产业的绿色协同。

安全。安全是人和社会的基本需要。元宇宙应实现用户层面的隐私安全、平台层面的数据安全和国家层面的国家安全相统一。

共赢。产业发展必须注重利益格局,共赢是元宇宙产业服务人类命运共同体的直接体现。平台与用户共赢、产业内共赢、国家间共赢是元宇宙产业乃至元宇宙文明的内在要求。

五　文明有序：元宇宙治理的中国方案

　　技术进步的方向和路径不是既定的，而是在已有技术、市场竞争、国家干预、伦理道德、法律制度等多种因素的作用下形成的。科学技术不会自然而然地导向善与福祉，只有加以引导和规范才能实现科技向善。未来的元宇宙是服务于人民群众，还是屈从于利益集团？是服务于全人类共同价值，还是屈从于西方国家霸权？是让人沉湎于精致的幻境，还是推动人类迈向星辰大海？路在何方？事在人为。

　　元宇宙发展不可能脱离元宇宙治理。治理天然具有公共性。在考虑治理问题时，既要在制度设计上着眼公共利益，也要确保输出的结果有利于公共利益。

　　当前，美国希望保持自己在全球网络治理的主导地位并将其延续至元宇宙治理，国外科技垄断巨头则依托市场争夺对元宇宙治理的影响力和话语权。以中国为代表的发展中国家具有强大的元宇宙增长动能，理应且必须提出超越国家霸权与资本霸权的元宇宙治理方案，切实维护人口占绝大多数而技术相对落后的广大发展中国家的权利和利益。元宇宙作为人类文明的新场域,理应且必须形成超越零和博弈与资本逻辑的人类文明新境界,向实现人的自由而全面发展迈进。

元宇宙治理的基础是尊重数字主权,方向是人类命运共同体,指南是全人类共同价值,原则是文明有序,路径是推动多边共治、实现共建共赢。

5.1 建设元宇宙文明的治理挑战

元宇宙必然存在外部性,即元宇宙必然给物理现实带来影响(副作用)。习近平总书记指出:"科技是发展的利器,也可能成为风险的源头。"[①] 如何处理好元宇宙必然存在的外部性,是前瞻元宇宙不可回避且应走在商业化元宇宙落地之前的重要问题。这种外部性主要表现为以下治理挑战:

认知障碍挑战。一方面,元宇宙中的全感官体验及数字人的存在与活动会对人的认知模式产生冲击,人不得不面对"他们是谁""他们是否属于人"的问题。另一方面,人的认知建立在感官体验的基础上,数字现实中的全感官体验可能使人迷失于元宇宙而无法将其与外部环境(物理现实)有效区分。因

---

① 《习近平谈治国理政》第 4 卷,北京:外文出版社,2022 年,第 201 页。

此，在构建元宇宙文明之初，就需要考虑数字人的身份问题及元宇宙与现实世界的优先级问题。

伦理道德挑战。元宇宙文明中必定形成有别于物理现实中的伦理道德，数字人的活动必定对既有伦理道德形成冲击。元宇宙在时间、空间和生理上突破人的固有限制，丰富人的存在形式，增强人的能力，拓展人的活动，满足人的需求，将从底层逻辑上重塑伦理道德。

权责界定挑战。元宇宙中的数字人有两个基本类别，一类是在物理现实中有对应本体的数字人，另一类是不存在本体的纯粹虚拟的数字人。当数字人在元宇宙中活动时，必定存在权利、义务和责任问题，也必定出现数字人之间的冲突问题。为了应对这种挑战，在界定数字人的基础上，还需要界定数字公民，并且根据数字人的类别明晰权责，确保数字人的行为可约束可追责。

文明冲突挑战。元宇宙中异质文明、异质文化之间的碰撞必定比互联网时代更加直接也更加激烈。当物理现实中经济利益、政治观点、宗教信仰等思想观念对立的人们在元宇宙中遭遇时，沉浸式的全感官体验所带来的冲击将远超互联网。化解这种冲突根本上需要在物理现实中构建人类命运共同体。如果考虑到让元宇宙成为人类命运共同体的先声，那么就需要构建一个公正的元宇宙社会体系，而不是将现存社会体制简单复刻到元宇宙中。

技术垄断挑战。西方发达国家和国际垄断资本必定希望将其技术垄断地位延续至未来的元宇宙文明中，以此实现元宇宙治理霸权和元宇宙中的剩余价值占有。技术垄断与人类命运共同体是根本背离的。为此，应当在元宇宙领域推动更加公平合理的国际技术标准治理体系，确保元宇宙平等地服务于所有接入者。

数字货币挑战。元宇宙中存在一整套与物理时空相互作用的经济体系，且必定存在与这一经济体系匹配的支付结算系统。目前，非同质化代币由于可以无摩擦地实现资金跨境流转而积累了一定的用户群体，甚至开始侵蚀传统主权货币。拥有技术优势的平台企业一旦主导元宇宙中的金融活动，必定对传统金融监管构成挑战。[①] 如果全球无法形成统一规制，那么跨国套利及洗钱等犯罪行为必定滋生。如果美国利用其传统网络霸权构建数字货币霸权，势必威胁广大发展中国家的利益。

数字主权挑战。习近平总书记指出，以信息技术为代表的新一轮科技和产业革命为经济社会发展注入强劲动力的同时，

[①] 袁曾：《元宇宙空间铸币权论》，《东方法学》2022年第2期。

互联网发展也给世界各国主权、安全、发展利益带来许多新的挑战。[①]互相尊重主权是全球治理体系的基本要求,也必然是元宇宙文明的基本要求。数字现实显然不会完全脱离于物理现实,因此,主权国家必定在元宇宙中存在数字主权诉求。追求人类命运共同体的元宇宙应当以尊重数字主权为前提,避免现存的霸权问题在元宇宙文明中重演。

内容安全挑战。霸权国家、极端主义、黑恶势力等必然试图利用元宇宙的高沉浸性来传播不良信息,元宇宙的经济系统也很可能带来洗钱、税基侵蚀与利润转移等问题,元宇宙的高实时性特点又给内容安全监管带来显著挑战。这些问题都需要通过顶层设计和技术底座协同来解决。

5.2 以文明有序的元宇宙走向元宇宙命运共同体

元宇宙是人类文明新场域,必定重塑人类文明。元宇宙治理由谁主导,以什么价值观为旗帜,关乎人类文明的未来。习近平总书记指出:"网络空间是人类共同的活动空间,网络空间前途命运应由世界各国共同掌握。各国应该加强沟通、扩大共

[①]《习近平关于网络强国论述摘编》,北京:中央文献出版社,2021年,第163页。

识、深化合作，共同构建网络空间命运共同体。"[1]

全人类共同价值是元宇宙文明的元价值。所谓元价值，就是反映价值观本质和内核的价值之魂。应以全人类共同价值为旗帜，携手构建网络空间命运共同体，推动网络空间命运共同体走向元宇宙命运共同体，使元宇宙成为人类命运共同体的先导。

每当人类文明走到重要关口，都需要先进思想和先进价值指引前进方向。2015年9月28日，习近平总书记出席第七十届联合国大会一般性辩论并发表重要讲话指出："和平、发展、公平、正义、民主、自由，是全人类的共同价值。"[2] 全人类共同价值以整体思维观照人类前途，主张在相互尊重、求同存异、文明互鉴的基础上形成价值最大公约数，为构建人类命运共同体凝聚价值共识，"做到发展共同推进、安全共同维护、治理共同参与、成果共同分享"[3]。

文明有序的元宇宙治理具有以下内涵：

尊重数字主权，反对霸权主义。一国政府是推动社会发展和维护社会秩序最核心的行动主体。尊重国家主权是国际交往的基本准则。国家主权范围具有历史性，当人类社会的生存空

---

[1]《习近平关于网络强国论述摘编》，北京：中央文献出版社，2021年，第155页。
[2]《习近平谈治国理政》第2卷，北京：外文出版社，2017年，第522页。
[3]《习近平关于网络强国论述摘编》，北京：中央文献出版社，2021年，第163页。

间拓展至互联网时，会催生网络主权。随着互联网向元宇宙的演化，网络主权必将升格为数字主权。建设和发展元宇宙应一改西方国家以霸权凌驾于主权之上的旧秩序，建立尊重数字主权、尊重国家间差异的元宇宙文明新秩序。

促进公平正义，超越数字垄断。公平正义是全人类长久以来的共同追求。科技巨头和大资本在网络空间的垄断、侵权、避税等顽疾是阻碍公平正义的绊脚石，受到全世界有识之士的质疑和批判。元宇宙治理必须建立超越资本逻辑和数字垄断的治理体制，元宇宙技术标准治理应避免少数科技巨头通过控制标准联盟、标准必要专利和专利池来牟取垄断利润的问题。

倡导多中心化，慎待去中心化。以区块链为代表的部分元宇宙底层技术的去中心化特征并不等价于治理的去中心化。从技术角度看，元宇宙的构建必定要满足许可、认证、兼容、互联等架构要求，这本身说明外部规制的必然性和可行性。从治理角度看，权威和治理中心是人类社会之必然："没有权威，就不可能有任何的一致行动。"[①] 因此，中心化不等于落后，去中心化不意味着先进。对去中心化治理的畅想某种程度上只是一种规范性主张，不代表实际趋势。事实上，治理的去中心化必

---

① 《马克思恩格斯文集》第 10 卷，北京：人民出版社，2009 年，第 372 页。

然有利于垄断资本和霸权国家。着眼于全世界最广大人民的利益，应当推进立足于尊重数字主权的多中心化治理。

主张平等尊重，维护共同生活。人民的获得感、幸福感、安全感是衡量元宇宙福祉的首要标准。一方面，获得感、幸福感、安全感源于多样化需求的充分满足，元宇宙治理必须以平等尊重的态度对待人类需求的多样性，并通过加强基础设施建设向相对落后的国家和地区普及元宇宙，实现平等接入元宇宙；另一方面，个体自由的边界是其他个体的自由，因此元宇宙治理不能对需求持放任态度，对多样化需求的满足必须以维护共同生活为前提。

明辨数实关系，构建良好秩序。元宇宙源于且基于现实社会，脱离现实社会提供的外部环境，元宇宙无从谈起。因此，要明辨数字现实和物理现实之间的优先级，确保任何元宇宙中的伦理道德法律不跃出物理现实的底线，避免元宇宙沦为法外之地。元宇宙同现实社会一样，既要尊重自由，也要保护秩序。自由是秩序的目的，秩序是自由的保障。要厘清物理现实中的自然人与其在不同类型的元宇宙中的数字分身之间的伦理和法律关系。根据具体应用场景中沉浸度和拟真度的不同，制定数字人行为准则。

共保数字安全，共享发展成果。元宇宙为人类生活带来美好体验及为经济发展带来新动能的同时,必定伴生全新的数字安全挑战。元宇宙中高水平的数实融合和人机融合也对数字安全提出更高的要求。筑牢元宇宙数字安全屏障不可能一蹴而就,必须由世界各国通力合作,强化顶层设计,完善制度规则、标准体系和配套政策,以数字安全保障全人类共享发展成果。

统筹全产业链,坚持绿色发展。环境问题和能源问题是人类面临的重大考验,环境关和能源关是元宇宙必须迈过去的门槛。尽管人类传递单位信息的排放和能耗在最近两百多年大大降低,但信息总量的爆炸式增长让总排放和总能耗大大提高。应当统筹元宇宙全产业链的绿色发展,通过技术进步和科学治理推动人类迈向绿色的信息文明。

共建元宇宙治理,共享元宇宙文明,走向元宇宙命运共同体,应重视议题首设原则和规则首创原则,避免被动跟随垄断资本和霸权国家预先设置的议题和预先创立的规则。

5.3 新时代元宇宙治理的政策原则

在推进元宇宙治理实现全人类共同价值的同时,还需要积极探索和布局我国的元宇宙治理,确立党管元宇宙的政治要求,实现从网络综合治理体系向元宇宙综合治理体系的演化,构建元宇宙法治,营造清朗元宇宙数字时空。以社会主义为根本原则的新时代元宇宙治理体系取得成功,必将让全世界看到元宇宙治理的中国智慧,进而在全球引领文明有序的元宇宙治理。

本研究尝试提出新时代元宇宙治理的如下政策原则:

坚持人民至上。"人民性是马克思主义的本质属性。"[1]建设、发展和治理元宇宙,归根结底是为了人民。尊重人民群众的智慧、创造和劳动成果,建设为人民所参与、所认同、所共享的元宇宙,避免资本至上、娱乐至上或技术至上的错误方向或片面观念。

坚持实践探索与理论创新共进。实践是理论的来源,是推动理论发展的根本动力,是检验真理的唯一标准;理论对实践具有能动的反作用,科学的理论可以引领实践。元宇宙发展初期,应当在实践上鼓励创新、鼓励发展,在理论上主动创新,形成实践与理论相辅相成的良好局面。

坚持顶层设计与技术底座协同。在元宇宙发展初期,应提早布局对底层架构的规制问题,通过顶层设计引导元宇宙治理

---

[1] 习近平:《高举中国特色社会主义伟大旗帜 为全面建设社会主义现代化国家而团结奋斗——在中国共产党第二十次全国代表大会上的报告》,北京:人民出版社,2022年,第19页。

体系，夯实元宇宙平台主体责任，明确用户主体责任，避免出现责任真空。

坚持正确处理政府与市场关系。在元宇宙发展初期，应处理好政府与市场的关系，避免新产业新业态兴起初期监管和法律缺位，在充分释放元宇宙产业市场活力的同时，建立规范的市场秩序。在坚持总体国家安全观的基础上，兼顾统筹发展和安全的双重目标，使党和政府在治理中发挥集中统一、高效权威的作用。

坚持数字经济与实体经济融合。党的二十大报告强调："坚持把发展经济的着力点放在实体经济上"，"加快发展数字经济，促进数字经济和实体经济深度融合，打造具有国际竞争力的数字产业集群"。[①] 元宇宙是数字经济发展的重要方向，是在新一轮科技革命背景下推动实体经济转型升级的重要力量。应当抓住数字经济与实体经济融合发展的关键机遇。

坚持产业壮大与技术引领配合。元宇宙全球治理的话语权和主导权既需要有强大的产业规模支持，又需要巩固的技术标准主导地位。因此必须发挥产业生态培育和核心技术研发的协同效应，特别是在底层核心技术研发和底层架构设计标准上实

---

① 习近平：《高举中国特色社会主义伟大旗帜 为全面建设社会主义现代化国家而团结奋斗——在中国共产党第二十次全国代表大会上的报告》，北京：人民出版社，2022年，第30页。

现引领地位。在元宇宙发展初期，就应注重自主创新和自主可控，强化元宇宙产业中的国家战略科技力量，发挥新型举国体制优势和超大规模市场优势，避免核心技术受制于人。

坚持风尚引领与法律规制并重。元宇宙中用户行为和内容生产的实时性给内容安全和内容监管带来技术挑战。作为数字现实空间，其基本治理机制可以对接并参照物理现实，形成贯穿内部和外部、事前和事后的治理体系。其一，通过物理现实中的教育和引领提高元宇宙用户素养；其二，引领元宇宙中的用户行为风尚，使数字人形成守序自觉；其三，制定和完善关于元宇宙的法律体系，依法治理无序乱序现象；其四，建立和完善元宇宙公共安全体系，应对高沉浸性、高实时性给元宇宙公共安全造成的挑战，使数字公民可以像物理现实中的公民一样得到公共安全保障。

坚持开放发展与维护安全协调。元宇宙必须走开放发展之路，而元宇宙的开放、实时和沉浸必然深刻改变承载价值体系的媒介、场景和内容，对元宇宙安全治理提出更高要求。应当推动形成积极引领、事前预防、安全监管和应急处置相统一，治理机制和治理效能相统一的元宇宙治理体系。

5.4 构建元宇宙文明生态系统

习近平总书记在首届中国网络文明大会上强调,网络文明建设"要坚持发展和治理相统一、网上和网下相融合,广泛汇聚向上向善力量"。在坚持全球互联网治理"四项原则"和"五点主张"的基础上,应构建以全人类共同价值为导向的元宇宙文明生态系统。

元宇宙文明生态系统应当坚持预防与惩治相统一,道德引导、法律规制和科技保障相统一,具体包括平台建设、应用开发、社区规则、经济系统和数字公民等五个维度:

完善平台建设。注重基于平台的元宇宙治理,从元宇宙平台的底层逻辑着眼完善元宇宙平台建设。

规范应用开发。在元宇宙应用开发上加强监管和引导,减少和避免那些可能破坏元宇宙文明生态和元宇宙治理的应用钻政策和法律漏洞。

引领社群自治。社群是社会治理的基本单元,也必定是元宇宙治理的基本单元。通过引领社群自治,充分调动数字公民的参与感、责任感和使命感。

创新经济系统。积极发展主权数字货币,探索新的货币流通规律和经济运行规律,加强数字资产保护,实现与物理时空中经济系统的良性互动。

塑造数字公民。让元宇宙中的数字人作为数字公民建设共同生活。倡导数字公民自觉遵守道德和法律，建立平等的社交关系和经济关系，构建良好的文明生态和有序的数字空间。

六 结语

在纪念马克思诞辰 200 周年大会上，习近平总书记着重指出："我们要赢得优势、赢得主动、赢得未来，必须不断提高运用马克思主义分析和解决实际问题的能力。"①

本研究着眼于元理论层次，追问元宇宙的根本。在元理论研究的基础上，尝试建构关于元宇宙的"中国自主的知识体系"，为我国及广大发展中国家在元宇宙的全球治理中争取话语权、主导权、议题设置权和规则制定权做理论探索。

6.1 如何理解元宇宙概念

社会各界对元宇宙概念的理解众说纷纭，不首先弄明白这个问题，就难免对元宇宙过度乐观或过度怀疑。本研究以辩证唯物主义和历史唯物主义为方法论，从科学技术进步和经济基础演化的角度考察了元宇宙的历史必然性和客观现实性，从三

---

① 《习近平谈治国理政》第 3 卷，北京：外文出版社，2020 年，第 74 页。

个视角定义元宇宙：

第一，元宇宙是技术聚合体、产业聚合体和生态聚合体；

第二，元宇宙是信息技术革命的愿景聚合；

第三，元宇宙是"人机物"三元融合的万物智能互联的系统。

上述三个视角均强调元宇宙概念的统合力：

其一，元宇宙不是具体的技术，而是众多技术系统的集成。这要求我们以全局思维和战略高度思考和布局元宇宙。但也需要意识到，元宇宙的很多具体目标是现有科技水平尚无法实现甚至还不够清晰的。

其二，元宇宙作为复杂系统，终究是由众多子系统构成，最终的形态和面貌是在发展中逐渐生成的；因此必须注重对各种具体技术和具体应用的布局，特别是涉及元宇宙底层逻辑的核心技术和关键系统。发展元宇宙不仅要靠战略规划，更要靠一项项具体的技术和应用。要着眼全局，也要重视落地问题。ChatGPT 的"风头"压过元宇宙，恰恰体现出落地的重要性。相比于元宇宙的统合性或综合性，ChatGPT 解决的是更具体的问题，尽管它存在很多局限，但落地终究更容易。这可能是近期 ChatGPT 在微软内部超越元宇宙部门的重要因素。这并不意味着元宇宙不可靠，而是提醒我们："合抱之木，生于毫末；

九层之台，起于累土。"支撑元宇宙的各种子技术，肯定比元宇宙先问世。必须重视长期积累的技术研发和市场开拓。能不能掌握元宇宙领域的话语权和主导权，归根结底还是看能否在国际竞争中掌握市场。无法主导技术路径，就无法主导技术标准；无法主导技术标准，就无法主导市场；无法主导市场，就无法主导治理。

其三，"元宇宙"作为语词，只是一个符号，指代着信息技术革命的愿景聚合。各个技术领域的累积性进步最终使"人机物"三元融合得以实现时，它未必真的就叫"元宇宙"。因此，元宇宙与人工智能并不是同一层次的概念。基于这样的认识，我们才不至于把元宇宙仅仅当成投资的风口，而是能看到，元宇宙概念融汇了信息技术革命将为人类文明带来的飞跃。

综上所述，认识和研判元宇宙，必须透过表象看本质。元宇宙是技术高地和产业高地，其背后是实在的技术、产业、应用和需求，因而是我国必争之地。

6.2 携手迈向元宇宙文明

人类正处于信息文明的初级阶段。新一轮科技革命和工业革命必然推动生产力飞跃，进而深刻变革生产方式、社会治理方式和全球治理体系，推动人类文明达到新境界。

当代全球治理体系中的国际组织、国际机构和国际规则主要是在第二次世界大战后由美西方主导建立的，代表性不足，包容性不够，被霸权逻辑和资本逻辑裹挟，不能充分体现广大发展中国家及全世界最广大人民的根本利益。特别是在新一轮科技革命和工业革命深入发展，世界格局加速演变的背景下，当代全球治理体系亟待变革。伴随着元宇宙的发展，人类能否以此为契机变革全球治理体系从而推动人类文明发展，真正实现人类命运共同体，是重要的时代课题。中国理应且能够为人类迈向信息文明高级阶段给出中国方案。

引领元宇宙治理，先要引领元宇宙发展。元宇宙是物理时空与数字时空交融的系统，因此应协同推进物理时空—数字时空"两手布局"，并坚持核心技术的自主可控。基础设施、硬件、终端、能源、环境、技术标准等是元宇宙的物质基础。当前，美国在半导体产业的"脱钩断链"已对我国高科技产业发展形成阻滞。没有高端半导体制造设备，就没有高端芯片；没有高端芯片，就无法搭建元宇宙的核心系统和交互系统，价值系统更无从谈起。必须坚持全局思维和系统思维，不投机、不短视，瞄准2050年全面建成社会主义现代化强国乃至更加高远的未来，使元宇宙成为人类实现自由而全面发展的阶梯。

参考文献

《马克思恩格斯文集》第 1 卷,北京:人民出版社,2009 年。
《马克思恩格斯文集》第 2 卷,北京:人民出版社,2009 年。
《马克思恩格斯文集》第 5 卷,北京:人民出版社,2009 年。
《马克思恩格斯文集》第 10 卷,北京:人民出版社,2009 年。
《马克思恩格斯全集》第 25 卷,北京:人民出版社,2001 年。
《马克思恩格斯全集》第 31 卷,北京:人民出版社,1998 年。
《马克思恩格斯全集》第 37 卷,北京:人民出版社,2019 年。
《习近平谈治国理政》第 2 卷,北京:外文出版社,2017 年。
《习近平谈治国理政》第 3 卷,北京:外文出版社,2020 年。
《习近平谈治国理政》第 4 卷,北京:外文出版社,2022 年。

习近平:《高举中国特色社会主义伟大旗帜 为全面建设社会主义现代化国家而团结奋斗——在中国共产党第二十次全国代表大会上的报告》,北京:人民出版社,2022 年。

《习近平关于网络强国论述摘编》,北京:中央文献出版社,2021 年。

习近平:《在网络安全和信息化工作座谈会上的讲话》,北京:人民出版社,2016年。

中华人民共和国国务院新闻办公室:《携手构建网络空间命运共同体》,中国政府网,2022年11月7日,http://www.gov.cn/zhengce/2022-11/07/content_5725117.htm。

《中国大百科全书》第23卷,北京:中国大百科全书出版社,2009年。

[德]H.哈肯:《信息与自组织:复杂系统的宏观方法》,郭治安译,成都:四川教育出版社,1988年。

[奥]L.贝塔兰菲:《一般系统论:基础·发展·应用》,秋同、袁嘉新译,北京:社会科学文献出版社,1987年。

[美]W. W.罗斯托:《这一切是怎么开始的——现代经济的起源》,黄其祥、纪坚博译,北京:商务印书馆,1997年。

段晓君、林益、赵城利编著:《系统科学教程》,北京:科学出版社,2019年。

高奇琦:《主权区块链与全球区块链研究》,《世界经济与政治》2020年第10期。

贾根良:《第三次工业革命与工业智能化》,《中国社会科学》2016年第6期。

刘大同、郭凯、王本宽等:《数字孪生技术综述与展望》,

《仪器仪表学报》2018年第11期。

吕廷杰、刘峰:《数字经济背景下的算力网络研究》,《北京交通大学学报(社会科学版)》2021年第1期。

[加]马歇尔·麦克卢汉:《理解媒介——论人的延伸》,何道宽译,北京:商务印书馆,2000年。

钱学森、宋健:《工程控制论》上册,北京:科学出版社,2011年。

任晓旭、谭靖超、邓辉等:《基于端边云超融合的算力网络架构》,《计算机应用》2022年第S1期。

司晓:《区块链数字资产物权论》,《探索与争鸣》2021年第12期。

孙柏林:《工业元宇宙——现实世界与虚拟世界互通的桥梁》,《计算机仿真》2022年第7期。

王轶辰:《元宇宙能过"能源关"吗》,《经济日报》2022年1月27日第6版。

吴国林主编《自然辩证法概论》,北京:清华大学出版社,2018年。

吴军:《全球科技通史》,北京:中信出版社,2019年。

闫同柱:《工业元宇宙就是下一张全真工业互联网》,《中国经贸导刊》2022年第6期。

袁园、杨永忠：《走向元宇宙：一种新型数字经济的机理与逻辑》，《深圳大学学报（人文社会科学版）》2022年第1期。

袁曾：《元宇宙空间铸币权论》，《东方法学》2022年第2期。

张瑜、闫聚群：《"网络文明"的概念辨析》，《青海社会科学》2014年第6期。

赵星、乔利利、叶鹰：《元宇宙研究与应用综述》，《信息资源管理学报》2022年第4期。

郑世林、陈志辉、王祥树：《从互联网到元宇宙：产业发展机遇、挑战与政策建议》，《产业经济评论》2022年第6期。

邹才能、何东博、贾成业等：《世界能源转型内涵、路径及其对碳中和的意义》，《石油学报》2021年第2期。

邹才能、赵群、张国生等：《能源革命：从化石能源到新能源》，《天然气工业》2016年第1期。

Alexander Hamilton. "Report on the Subject of Manufactures (1791)," Frank W. Taussig, ed., *State Papers and Speeches on the Tariff*, Cambridge, MA: Harvard University, 1892.

Barry Collins, "The Metaverse: How to Build a Massive Virtual World," *Forbes*, https://www.forbes.com/, Sep 25, 2021.

Claude Elwood Shannon, "A Mathematical Theory of Communication," *The Bell System Technical Journal*, vol.27, no.3,

1948.

Enis Karaarslan & Mohammed Babiker, "Digital Twin Security Threats and Countermeasures: An Introduction," 2021 International Conference on Information Security and Cryptology (ISCTURKEY), IEEE, 2021.

Ilya Prigogine, "Time, Structure and Fluctuations," *Science*, 1978, vol.201, no.4358, pp. 777-785.

Jeremy Rifkin, *The Empathic Civilization: The Race to Global Consciousness in a World in Crisis*, Penguin, 2009.

John D.N. Dionisio, William G. Burns III & Richard Gilbert, "3D Virtual Worlds and the Metaverse: Current Status and Future Possibilities," *ACM Computing Surveys* (CSUR), 2013, vol.45, no.3, pp. 1-38.

John Herrman & Kellen Browning, "Are We in the Metaverse Yet?" *The New York Times*, Jul 10, 2021.

Kim Jooyoung, "Advertising in the Metaverse: Research Agenda," *Journal of Interactive Advertising*, 2021, vol.21, no.3, pp. 141-144.

Preface (I)

Since the beginning of the 21st century, global technological innovation has been extraordinarily active. The new generation of information technology, represented by mobile communications, artificial intelligence, the Internet of Things, quantum information, and blockchain technology, is accelerating breakthroughs, restructuring the global innovation landscape, and reshaping the global economic structure. On November 9, 2022, General Secretary Xi Jinping indicated in his congratulatory letter to the 2022 World Internet Conference Wuzhen Summit that in today's era, digital technology, as the leading force in the world's scientific revolution and industrial transformation, is increasingly integrating into the entire process of economic and social development, profoundly changing production methods, lifestyles, and social

governance methods. As a future vision of the information technology revolution, the metaverse is both a vast blue ocean for China's state-owned enterprises and a valuable opportunity for the innovative development of Marxism.

Marxism is a historical science that adapts to constantly changing conditions and must evolve with changes in reality. The rapidly changing science, technology, and economic production are fertile soil for Marxism. Faced with new phenomena and problems, we should not expect to find ready-made answers from the classics, nor should we copy and follow Western theories. Marxism maintains its integrity and innovation by adhering to Marxist scientific methodology and building a Chinese Independent Knowledge System based on practice. Our collaboration with Migu Culture Technology Limited Company to establish a joint research center and conduct collaborative research is precise to root ourselves in China better, tell Chinese stories, develop Chinese theories, and serve Chinese practice.

Marxism is a scientific theory, a people's theory, a

practical theory, and a constantly developing open theory. Deepening Marxist research and promoting innovation and breakthroughs in Chinese-style modernization in theory and practice can only be achieved by participating in and comprehending the dynamic Chinese method. The cutting-edge research on the metaverse-related fundamental theory jointly carried out by the Tsinghua University (School of Marxism) and Migu Culture Technology Limited Company is a reasonable attempt to persist in combining the basic principles of Marxism with China's specific realities and to advance the sinicization and modernization of Marxism continuously. During the research process, researchers from both sides fully exploited their respective strengths, held several focused discussions, repeatedly polished the report's content, made significant progress in understanding and applying Marxism, and grasped the development of information technology and its industry, achieving a synergistic effect of 1+1>2 and exploring a new path of cooperation between schools and enterprises.

The metaverse is a new phenomenon and is in the

process of rapid development and change. Forward-looking research on the metaverse has strategic significance, but due to time and level constraints, there may inevitably be omissions or errors. We welcome valuable criticism, opinions, and suggestions from readers, especially peers from academia and industry.

Zhu Andong

November 9, 2022, at Tsinghua University Campus, Beijing

Preface (II)

Human society is accelerating into the era of an information civilization. Information and energy, the two main drivers of human civilization's progress, are evolving from relatively independent development to mutual integration and innovation. As a representative industry and new track of the digital economy, the metaverse has been a buzzword in the industry for several years now. It has become the strategic frontier of the digital economy.

China Mobile focuses on the world-class "Power Mansion" strategy and implements the "1225 Strategy", expanding into cutting-edge fields such as the metaverse. Migu Culture Technology Limited Company (hereinafter referred to as "Migu") started the practical exploration and path research of the metaverse relatively early and is committed to the deep integration of industry, academia, and research, improving the level of technological achievements transformation and industrialization.

The "Power Mansion" strategy aims to create a world-class enterprise by promoting digital transformation and high-quality development. The plan emphasizes party building, integration, and serving various market segments, including individuals, households, governments, enterprises, and emerging markets.

The "1225 Strategy" is China Mobile's long-term strategic plan, focusing on two key transformations: shifting from an emphasis on quantity and scale to prioritizing quality, efficiency, and effectiveness; and transitioning from short-term performance to long-term value growth. The plan also incorporates the development of new information infrastructure and service systems and aims to tap into potential benefits from innovation, public sentiment, reform, talent, and ecology.

To further explore the construction and civilization of the metaverse, in 2022, Migu and Tsinghua University (School of Marxism) jointly established the Joint

Research Center for Intelligent Party Building and Ideological and Political Education (hereinafter referred to as "JCIPPE") and released the report "Metatheory Study of the Metaverse". The purpose is to explore fundamental theoretical issues such as the worldview, methodology, values, and corresponding discourse system of the metaverse and to construct a "Chinese Independent Knowledge System" about the metaverse under the larger theoretical system of Marxism.

In the context of pursuing the shared values of all humanity and building a community with a shared future for mankind, "what the metaverse should be" is an essential theoretical issue with strategic and global significance. The establishment of the JCIPPE aims to maximize the value of the metaverse, making it a digital space for realizing the shared values of all humanity and an integral approach to promoting the construction of a community with a shared future for mankind.

Exploring the Chinese-style metaverse innovation model is significant for promoting the digital

transformation of thousands of industries and meeting people's need for a better life. Migu will fully leverage its advantages in 5G+ computing power networks, follow the "Metaverse MIGU Evolution Roadmap", and join hands with partners from all walks of life to create a new metaverse ecosystem with Chinese characteristics through "content + technology + integrated innovation", contributing to the construction of a strong cybernation, Digital China, and intelligent society, and contributing Chinese standards, Chinese solutions, and Chinese strength to global industrial development.

As spring blossoms and all things grow, we present this book on the fundamental theory of the metaverse to our readers, hoping it can provide a reference for exploring the future of the metaverse. Due to limited time and the ever-evolving nature of research, this book will inevitably have omissions and need to be revised. We welcome your criticism and corrections.

Liu Xin

April, 2023

Introduction: Contributing Chinese Wisdom to the Metaverse Civilization

We are witnesses and participants in a new round of technological revolution. On May 28, 2021, General Secretary Xi Jinping, in his speech at the 20th Academician Conference of the Chinese Academy of Sciences, the 15th Academician Conference of the Chinese Academy of Engineering, and the 10th National Congress of the China Association for Science and Technology, pointed out that currently, "the speed of technological innovation has significantly been accelerated. Emerging technologies such as information technology and artificial intelligence are developing rapidly, greatly expanding the scope of time, space, and human cognition. Humanity is entering an era of the intelligent interconnection of all things, integrating humans, machines, and objects."[1] This is the primary judgment of the Party Central Committee on the general trend of the new round of technological

revolution we are currently facing.

The new round of technological revolution will inevitably promote systemic changes in human society. The rapid progress of cutting-edge technologies such as quantum technology, big data, cloud computing, extended reality, and artificial intelligence is pushing the relationship between humans and nature, humans and society, and even humans and themselves toward a critical point of change from quantitative to qualitative. While technological progress brings unprecedented abundance and efficiency to humanity, it also carries risks and hidden dangers in the areas of the economy, ethics, emotions, and security. Moreover, the inherent contradictions of the capitalist system have never allowed the achievements of the productivity revolution since the second half of the 18th century to be shared by all humanity. Whether we can reform the unjust and unreasonable global governance system and make the fruits of the new round of technological revolution fully benefit all humanity is a significant issue that urgently needs to be resolved by the international community.

In this regard, China is responsible and able to contribute Chinese wisdom and strength. On November 9, 2022, General

Secretary Xi Jinping sent a congratulatory letter to the 2022 World Internet Conference Wuzhen Summit, stating, "In today's era, digital technology, as the leading force of the world's technological revolution and industrial transformation, is increasingly integrated into the entire process of economic and social development, profoundly changing production methods, lifestyles, and social governance methods. Faced with the opportunities and challenges brought about by digitalization, the international community should strengthen dialogue and communication, deepen practical cooperation, and work together to build a more fair, reasonable, open, inclusive, secure, stable, and vibrant cyberspace.... China is willing to join hands with countries around the world to embark on a global digital development path that features shared construction and sharing of digital resources, a vibrant digital economy, precise and efficient digital governance, prosperous development of digital culture, strong digital security assurance, and mutually beneficial and win-win digital cooperation, accelerating the construction of a community of shared future in cyberspace, and contributing wisdom and strength to world peace and development and human civilization progress." This is the Chinese answer to the major question of where humanity is heading in the context of the new round of technological revolution and the resulting widespread social changes.

The 20th National Congress of the Communist Party of China report called for accelerating the construction of cyber power and digital China, positioning new-generation information technology and artificial intelligence as new growth engines, and emphasized the need to accelerate the development of the digital economy, promote the deep integration of the digital economy and the real economy, and create internationally competitive digital industry clusters. This is the strategic positioning of the digital economy under the overall task of the Chinese Path to Modernization.

As a future vision of the information technology revolution, the metaverse is integral to the cyber power and digital China puzzle. It is bound to be the material foundation for achieving the Chinese Path to Modernization, promoting the construction of a community with a shared future for mankind, and creating new forms of human civilization. However, developing countries, including China, still need to form a leading role in technology and ideas for the latest trend and phenomena of the metaverse. This means that the current unjust and unreasonable phenomena in global cyberspace governance and hegemonic, domineering, and bullying behaviors may be derived into the global governance of the metaverse.

The right to interpret, construct, and govern the metaverse, as well as the right to set the agenda and make rules, should and must be in the hands of the Chinese people themselves. This requires us to engage in forward-looking exploration actively. Currently, it is a time of unprecedented changes in a century. How to understand the metaverse from the perspective of achieving the Chinese Path to Modernization and building a community with a shared future for mankind, and whether China can propose and explore a solution leading to a community with a shared future for mankind in this new world of the metaverse, are the research background and core concerns of this report.

To make a Chinese voice and provide Chinese solutions for developing the metaverse, we need the support of scientific theories. General Secretary Xi Jinping pointed out, "accelerating the construction of philosophy and social sciences with Chinese characteristics is ultimately about constructing Chinese Independent Knowledge System." The core purpose of this study is to explore

the "Chinese Independent Knowledge System" concerning the metaverse, specifically, to construct a worldview, methodology, values, and corresponding discourse system about the metaverse and to make theoretical explorations for our country and the vast majority of developing countries to strive for the right to speak, lead, set the agenda, and make rules in the global governance of the metaverse.

Chapter 1
Metaverse Research Overview

When we talk about the metaverse, what exactly are we discussing? This is the first question that needs to be clarified in metaverse research. In domestic and international public opinions and academic circles, some believe the metaverse is merely a gimmick created for commercial hype. Since the release of ChatGPT in November, 2022, many observers have asserted that the metaverse is nothing more than a fading trend. Understanding the metaverse is the foundation for exploring the "Chinese Independent Knowledge System" about the metaverse.

1.1 Metaversology and its Metatheory

Exploring the "Chinese Independent Knowledge System" about the metaverse essentially is to explore China's independent metaversology. This requires us to consider the following questions:

First, what is metaversology?

Second, what is the research object of metaversology?

Third, where are the boundaries of metaversology? That is the scope of research.

Fourth, how do we study the metaverse and the research methods?

Metaversology refers to various theories or doctrines about the metaverse. It is an abstract product of human thinking about various specific phenomena in the metaverse. Numerous papers and monographs on the metaverse produced in recent years are the literature of metaversology.

The research object of metaversology is the metaverse as an objective existence or objective trend, which includes various manifestations and phenomena of the metaverse, as well as the objective evolutionary trends of these phenomena, such as the progress of computing networks, the advancement of artificial intelligence, the popularization of digital currencies, and the development of digital competitive sports.

The scope of metaversology research depends on how many

fields the research object involves. Metaversology is a theoretical blue ocean covering numerous knowledge areas in natural sciences, philosophy, and social sciences.

The research methods of metaversology cannot be generalized. Generally speaking, research methods include two levels: one is the methodology at the abstract level, which refers to the general principles of thought on how to understand and study the metaverse; the other level involves various specific research methods, such as case studies, comparative studies, etc. The former guides the latter, and the latter expresses the former.

Metaversology research in different disciplinary fields has different specific research methods due to the different research objects. However, for China's independent metaversology, the methodology should be unified, namely with dialectical materialism and historical materialism. In April, 2018, General Secretary Xi Jinping pointed out during the Fifth Collective Study of the 19th Central Political Bureau that "the scientific and revolutionary nature of Marxist theory stems from the scientific worldview and methodology of dialectical materialism and historical materialism, which provide us with a powerful ideological weapon to understand

and transform the world" and emphasized focusing on the "major practical issues in China's reform and opening up and socialist modernization." Studying the metaverse certainly requires examining the laws of scientific and technological development, which requires the guidance of dialectical materialism, while the metaverse and its governance also involve social and historical laws—such as economic laws and social governance laws—which require the guidance of historical materialism.

The above content, including research objects, research scope, research methods, etc., constitutes the basic problems of metaversology. How these questions are answered determines the specific views that will be formed in a particular metaverse study. The sum of these basic questions constitutes the metatheory of metaversology. "Metatheory" is not a "theory of the metaverse" but refers to a theory about a particular theory, a term used to describe the foundational theory of a discipline.

The metaverse, metaversology, and metatheory of metaversology represent three levels, which transition from concrete to abstract and objective reality to theoretical thinking. Among them, the metaverse is the research object of metaversology, and metaversology is the research object of the metatheory of metaversology. The sum of various theoretical studies on the metaverse as an objective trend forms metaversology; the theoretical abstraction of the basic problems of metaversology further forms the metatheory of metaversology.

1.2 Metaverse Concept

To explore China's independent metaversology, it is necessary to establish an independent understanding of the metaverse concept. To understand the metaverse, one must look beyond appearances to the essence. Some views argue that the metaverse is nothing more than a concept hyped by capital for speculation; others argue that the metaverse is a strategy for digital capitalism to evade dilemmas by creating concepts. Based on the methodology of dialectical materialism and historical materialism, examining the metaverse concept ultimately involves determining whether this concept reflects the objective trend of scientific and technological progress and economic and social development.

Focusing on scientific and rigorous perspectives, there is

currently no need to provide an overly precise definition of the metaverse because the specific form of a mature metaverse depends on a considerable period of future technological progress and economic and social development. We only need to grasp the metaverse's basic nature and trends. This is a scientific attitude. Although scientific theories certainly have a predictive function, predictions must be made with appropriate scope.

Based on the above principles, this report defines the metaverse from three perspectives:

First, the metaverse is a technological, industrial, and ecological aggregate. In other words, the metaverse is a complex system formed by aggregating numerous technologies, industries, and ecologies, which is underpinned by tangible technology clusters, industry clusters, and user demand.

Second, the metaverse is the vision aggregation of the information technology revolution. The metaverse concept has attracted global attention fundamentally because, in the past, in the field of information technology, mobile communication technology, cloud computing technology, virtual reality technology, and blockchain technology may have described their respective future scenarios, but all focused only on a particular branch of the information technology revolution. The metaverse concept successfully paints a complete vision of the information technology revolution for people, making the roles and positions of various existing technologies and technology directions in the future society's puzzle suddenly clear.

Third, the metaverse is a system of intelligent interconnection of all things through the fusion of "human-machine-object". From the perspective of the fusion of "human-machine-object", the core of the metaverse concept can be understood as the construction of space and time. Time and space are the fundamental dimensions of human practical activities. The development of information technology has given humans increasingly powerful space-time construction capabilities, enabling the creation of a digital world (digital space-time) that replicates the real world (physical space-time) through technologies such as digital twins. However, a clear boundary still exists between digital space-time and the real world, as it lacks independent time and cannot provide a full sensory experience; it merely serves as a supplement, extension, and attachment to physical space-time. With the advancement of

information technology, particularly the development of artificial intelligence toward brain and cognitive intelligence, the metaverse is expected to provide a full sensory experience and have a complete economic and social system capable of reproduction activities. If these are realized, the metaverse will present itself in a realistic rather than virtual form, becoming a digital space-time that blends with the physical space-time. The essence of the metaverse is to construct a digital space-time that is native to and interwoven with physical space-time.

1.3 Metaverse Civilization

Civilization is "the sum of material, institutional and spiritual achievements created by human beings in their activities of understanding and transforming the world, and is the basic symbol of socio-historical progress and the state of human enlightenment."[2] Seen statically, civilization encompasses all the progressive achievements created by human society; viewed dynamically, civilization represents the evolutionary process of human society.[3]

The development of the metaverse will inevitably give birth to a metaverse civilization. The metaverse represents tangible technology clusters, industry clusters, and user demand, so its development will inevitably promote the evolution of human society. The sum of all progressive achievements created by humans in this evolutionary process constitutes the metaverse civilization.

Since the birth of human civilization, primitive civilization, agricultural civilization, and industrial civilization have successively evolved. Information and communication technology development since the 1940s and 1950s has propelled human society toward an information civilization. General Secretary Xi Jinping pointed out: "Looking at the history of social development, humans have experienced agricultural and industrial revolutions and are currently undergoing an information revolution."[4] This is the understanding of the revolutionary role of technological progress from the perspective of social history and the history of civilization. Based on historical materialism, the contradiction between productive forces and production relations constitutes the fundamental driving force for the evolution of civilization. The forms and manifestations of culture, philosophy, law, politics, and the state ultimately depend on the level of productive forces (technological level): "Hand mills produce feudal societies, steam mills produce industrial capitalist societies."[5]

The metaverse civilization is an advanced stage of the information civilization. From a macro-historical perspective, modern humans are still in the initial stage of the information civilization, or network civilization. The achievements of network civilization manifest economically in the advancement of production methods and collaboration, the diversification and expansion of communication methods, and politically in the improvement of administrative efficiency, the expansion of social participation, and the popularization of e-government. Culturally, it is reflected in the expansion of knowledge dissemination, the development of cultural innovation, and the enrichment of spiritual life content.[6] The continuous breakthroughs and integrated development of information technology will truly usher humanity into the era of the intelligent interconnection of all things through the fusion of "human-machine-object", forming a civilization form that blends physical space-time and digital space-time based on human space-time construction capabilities. This will evolve the information civilization from its initial stage to an advanced stage, i.e., the metaverse civilization.

The intersection of digital space-time and physical space-time is the hallmark of metaverse civilization. Before the metaverse civilization, digital space-time could be constructed in certain scenarios, but it was not well-developed. There was no mention of digital space-time in agricultural and industrial civilizations. Although digital space-time built using information technology exists in network civilization, a clear boundary remains between virtual and reality, and digital space-time is only a supplement, extension, and attachment to physical space-time in terms of functionality and logic. Therefore, before the advent of the metaverse civilization, physical space-time was the absolute center of human civilization. Most activities and phenomena in cyberspace revolve around people's activities in physical space-time. The metaverse civilization is different, as it expands the center of human civilization from physical space-time to digital space-time; in other words, human civilization will acquire a form that blends physical and digital space-time.

1.4 Metaverse Construction and Governance

To move toward the metaverse civilization, it is essential to coordinate metaverse construction and governance.

From a systems theory perspective, metaverse construction includes core, interaction, and value systems.

First, the core system includes infrastructure and subsystems that support the metaverse. The infrastructure consists of computing networks and digital engines. The computing network is a fusion of multiple innovative technologies represented by 5G, including 5G, artificial intelligence, blockchain technology, cloud computing, big data, networking, edge computing, terminals, and security. Its goal is to achieve ubiquitous networks, omnipresent computing power, and pervasive intelligence. The digital engine is the core driver of the digital upgrade of industries, promoting the digital transformation of various fields. Relying on various underlying technologies, subsystems are formed to support the metaverse, including space-time construction systems (computing systems and ubiquitous intelligence), rule construction systems (credit systems, digital property rights, civilized ecology), and application security systems (data security, privacy security, etc.).

Second, the interaction system refers to the media, scenarios, and content that incorporate the metaverse and enable it to interact with humans, supported by the infrastructure. Media, scenarios, and content are the three elements of the interaction system. Various terminals and application platforms of the metaverse belong to the media. Different terminals and application platforms form metaverse scenarios catering to different needs, presenting different content in various metaverse scenarios. The media determines the logic and form of digital-physical integration, i.e., how people shuttle[7] between physical space-time and digital space-time, how they engage in metaverse activities, how scenarios are constructed, and how content is presented. All practical activities in the metaverse are generally realized through interactions with media, scenarios, and content.

Third, the value system includes two aspects: on the one hand, it is the values people hold in constructing the metaverse and developing metaverse civilization, which will directly affect the rule construction system and application security system of the metaverse and play a crucial role in building the interaction system. This means that we must carefully consider what kind of metaverse do we expect? A metaverse that helps achieve free and comprehensive human development, or one full of exploitation, deception, violence, and security risks? On the other hand, the value system also involves the value concepts inevitably contained in all activities within the metaverse. All practical activities of people in the metaverse will leave imprints on themselves and the metaverse, shaping their own value concepts and affecting others' value concepts. Value concepts are not innate or fixed but are formed and continuously shaped through human practice, influenced by both one and others and the environment. In this sense, "the medium is the message,"[8] and the message is the concept —media, scenarios, and content are both influenced by and shape values, affecting both the value concepts of the actors and those of others. Therefore, metaverse construction must first answer the questions of where the metaverse is heading and whom it serves.

The distinction between the three systems mentioned above implies that the underlying logic of the metaverse is a combination of technology and value norms. Currently, the metaverse is still in its infancy, with diverse technological paths and an unclear future.

It will inevitably undergo a long accumulation process, trial and error, and competition in the international market. The future of the metaverse depends directly on market competition, and the success of metaverse products in market competition depends on whether their infrastructure is sufficiently sound, their interaction systems are sufficiently developed, and their value systems resonate with people.

As a typical application of information technology, the metaverse inevitably exhibits network effects. Network effects refer to the degree to which a product meets user needs to be related to the scale of the social network within the product. The more users there are, the greater the value each user can derive from the social network. Building metaverse application scenarios, formulating governance rules, and advocating for a civilized metaverse ecosystem ultimately need to address whether users will come and accept them. Without a sufficiently large user base, there can be no discourse, leadership, agenda-setting, or rule-making power. Conversely, companies may tacitly accept or even cater to content involving curiosity, vulgarity, pornography, and violence to attract users in a competitive market. Therefore, effective guidance and

regulation are indispensable in building the metaverse; otherwise, capital expansion is likely to become chaotic.

Thus, the value system of the metaverse holds a pivotal position. If the leading position in the construction of the metaverse is lost in the value system, even if achievements are made in the core system and interaction system, it will be difficult to ensure industrial and ideological security, let alone meet General Secretary Xi Jinping's requirements for the "three common goals" of technological innovation.[9]

1.5 Metatheory Research on the Metaverse

The more revolutionary the potential impact of new technologies and industries, the less viable a following strategy is, and the more necessary it is to have independent foresight, theoretical exploration, strategic planning, and scientific guidance.

Whether the metaverse civilization can satisfy people's aspirations worldwide for a better life is not merely a technical or economic issue. It also involves factors such as ethics, national governance, international competition, technological innovation, and energy supply. It is a highly complex systemic issue. Building a community with a shared future for mankind and realizing the common values of all humanity are intrinsic to a metaverse civilization. During the 39th Collective Study Session of the Political Bureau of the Central Committee, General Secretary Xi Jinping emphasized to, "promote the common values of all humanity contained in Chinese civilization and promote the building of a community with a shared future for mankind". Chinese civilization should pave the way for every individual's free and comprehensive development in the metaverse civilization.

General Secretary Xi Jinping stressed "to adhere to and develop socialism with Chinese characteristics, we must attach great importance to the role of theory."[10] Time is of the essence; to lead the metaverse civilization, we must grasp the "essence" of theoretical research and fundamentally dissect the metaverse. Only in this way can we fully understand the top-level design of the metaverse and fully recognize the opportunities and potential challenges it holds. Therefore, this report delves into the metatheory level, attempting to establish coordinates for China's independent metaverse studies and metaverse development to build a community

with a shared future for mankind.

This report is not to discuss the basic issues and fundamental theories of metaverse studies in a general sense. Instead, it attempts to construct a "Chinese Independent Knowledge System" about the metaverse over the basic issues and at the fundamental theories level. Therefore, this report is titled "Metatheory Research on the Metaverse". Under this theme, the report mainly examines the metaverse from four aspects: historical inevitability, objective reality, value norms, and governance of public interest.

Using dialectical materialism and historical materialism as the methodology, this study first examines whether the metaverse concept is merely a marketing tactic or a genuine objective trend. This involves studying the metaverse's historical inevitability and objective reality, researching where it comes from and why it exists and corresponding to Chapters 2 and 3 of this report.

The development of the metaverse is more than just a technical issue. When any technology is applied to society, it inevitably gives rise to ethical, normative, and governance issues. In an ontological sense, the metaverse is a creation of human practice: human society came first, followed by the metaverse. What does this imply? On the one hand, the metaverse cannot develop in isolation and must be in harmony with the real world. This is not an issue that can be resolved solely within the metaverse industry; it requires the support of national strategies, industrial policies, and infrastructure investments. On the other hand, if the development of the metaverse interferes with and undermines economic and social development and civilizational progress, it indicates a reversal of priorities and a focus on the trivial at the expense of the essential. Therefore, the metaverse must be included to develop, and we must pay attention to issues of values and governance. This involves studying the metaverse's value norms and governance of public interest, answering the questions of where the metaverse is heading, and whom it serves, corresponding to Chapters 4 and 5 of this report.

Chapter 2
Spatiotemporal Construction: Insights from the History of Science and Technology

How can the metaverse be defined? Based on dialectical materialism and historical materialism, we need to examine whether the metaverse concept reflects an objective existence or trend to answer this question. This involves understanding the metaverse from the perspective of the objective laws of scientific and technological progress and economic and social development.

Although the metaverse concept originated from science fiction and is currently mainly an integration of existing technologies, the technology system, paradigm, and innovation trends it represents are real. The inevitability and reality of the metaverse are rooted in the objective laws of scientific and technological progress. Therefore, the metaverse is not a false concept; conversely, if we do not insist on understanding and defining the metaverse based on the objective laws of scientific and technological progress, our understanding of the metaverse may easily slide into fantasy.

Matter, energy, and information are the basic elements of nature. From the perspective of the relationship between humans and nature, the history of science and technology is the history of humans' increasingly recognizing and exploiting matter, energy, and information. We can examine the metaverse's historical inevitability and objective reality based on these three dimensions: matter, energy, and information.

2.1 The Metaverse as a Human-Made Material System

Dialectical materialism believes that systems are the forms of existence of all matter in nature. Ludwig von Bertalanffy, one of the founders of general systems theory, defines a system as a "set of interrelated elements"[11], while noted Chinese rocket scientist Qian Xuesen defines a system as a "whole with a specific function, organized by various parts that are mutually constrained"[12].

Based on whether a system has a priori existence relative to human society, we can distinguish between natural systems and human-made systems. Celestial bodies, oceans, and ecosystems are all natural systems. Human-made systems exist within natural systems and are the products of human practice. Mobile phones, the Internet, and cities are all human-made systems. If the concept of the metaverse becomes a reality, then the metaverse would also be a human-made system.

Systems are not only material forms of existence but also undergo evolution. The evolutionary process in which a system spontaneously forms an ordered structure due to the interaction of its internal elements or subsystems, without external instructions, is called self-organization.[13] Lasers, cells, ecosystems, human societies, and the earth all belong to self-organized systems.

Openness is a prerequisite for system evolution. An open system exchanges matter and energy with its environment at its boundaries. Only when the exchange of matter and energy with the outside world drives the open system away from equilibrium, with the negative entropy flow greater than entropy increase, can the system potentially transform into dissipative structures, nurturing new structures and achieving evolution?[14] As theoretical physicist Ilya Romanovich Prigogine states, "Non-equilibrium may be a source of order."[15]

Human social development is a typical example of an open system's self-organization. Practice is how human society and nature exchange matter and energy. The inexhaustible driving force propels human society as an open system away from equilibrium. Among all forms of practice, the driving force of science and technology is the most powerful——Marx considered science to be "a great historical lever"[16] and the ultimate revolutionary force.

The development of information technologies such as mobile communications, augmented reality, artificial intelligence, big data, and digital engines has made the fusion of "human-machine-object" human-made material systems a predictable trend. Current cyberspace is only a supplement, extension, and accessory to physical space-time and cannot exist without instructions from physical space-time. The metaverse realizes the integration of digital space-time and physical space-time based on the fusion of "human-machine-object". In this sense, human will is no longer an external instruction but an internal element of the system. In this sense, the metaverse can also be understood as a concept describing the future operating characteristics of human society from the perspective of integrating digital and physical space-time.

2.2 The Metaverse as an Indicator of Energy Utilization Levels

Energy is the ability of a physical system to do work. Energy is essential for human survival and all practical activities. Only by first obtaining and utilizing energy can we transform the environment, produce products, transmit information, and establish organizations. Based on the use of energy, humans have engaged in increasingly advanced production activities, which in turn support increasingly diverse social lives and increasingly developed cultural forms.

Energy comes from the development and utilization of energy resources. Energy resources are carriers that can directly or indirectly provide energy and are the material basis of human civilization. Almost all the energy needed for the operation of contemporary human society is essentially solar energy. The Neolithic Agricultural Revolution made biomass energy the earliest energy source to be developed and utilized in human history. The Industrial Revolution, which began in the mid-18th century and centered on the large-scale application of steam power, led humans into the Steam Age. The Second Industrial Revolution in the 1860s brought humanity into the Electric Age. Electricity became a new form of power, enabling mass production and consumption and greatly strengthening the socialization of capitalist production. Moreover, this revolution began with the rich material life of contemporary humans based on electricity. Therefore, the Second Industrial Revolution is also called the Electric Revolution. The Third Industrial Revolution, which began in the 1940s and 1950s, further enhanced humanity's energy utilization levels. From nuclear energy to various clean energy sources, electricity gained a more extensive and abundant energy foundation. With electricity as a prerequisite, computer technology and information and communication technology flourished and enabled humans to establish cyberspace.

Improvements in energy utilization levels have always accompanied major advances in human civilization. On the one hand, when the energy utilization level reaches a new stage, humans have the conditions to obtain new forms of power and use them to develop and drive new means of production. On the other hand, the growing needs of human society's production and life inevitably promote the progress of energy utilization levels.[17]

Looking at the development laws of energy utilization levels, the metaverse has already begun to show its objective reality. Firstly, the continuous increase of energy density and the development of energy quality from high-carbon to low-carbon are the general trends of world energy development.[18] At present, breakthroughs in clean energy development are being made, and controllable nuclear fusion is expected to achieve an endless and environmentally friendly energy supply. In 2020, the new generation of controllable nuclear fusion research device China's HL-2M Tokamak was completed and successfully discharged. Once humans master controllable nuclear fusion technology, they can make the "artificial sun" dream a reality, supporting the massive power consumption required to construct the metaverse. Secondly, only with a clean, stable, and inexhaustible energy supply can computing power stably drive the power of the metaverse. Windmills and wind turbines belong to wind power mechanical systems, watermills and hydro turbines are hydraulic mechanical systems, and steam engines and internal combustion engines are thermal mechanical systems. The metaverse is a material system established by humans based on integrating digital and physical space-time. Its power is supported by computing power systems that rely on the electrical power provided by physical space-time. Therefore, the metaverse will be the fruit of the breakthrough in energy utilization levels in the next technological revolution.

Of course, the energy utilization level required for the metaverse still faces significant challenges.[19] Although the "New Energy Revolution" is accelerating, humanity's development and energy utilization since the Second Industrial Revolution have not yet achieved disruptive progress comparable to steam engines and electricity. A highly developed level of energy utilization is the absolute material prerequisite for the metaverse. To achieve a metaverse experience like those depicted in science fiction novels like *Snow Crash* and movies like *Ready Player One* both an energy technology revolution and a computing power revolution driven by hardware and software are needed. This would support more powerful computing power with lower energy consumption to cope with the dramatic increase in data density.

2.3 Metaverse as a Representation of Information Transmission Levels

Information reflects the way elements within a system are connected. Information is not material, but its existence relies on a medium or carrier; information itself has no energy, but its transmission requires energy. From the perspective of information theory, information is the reduction of uncertainty.[20] Information is required everywhere, from sound to text, science, and technology to culture and art, and collaboration to national governance.

The evolution of material systems from simple to complex is a process of entropy reduction and information increase. The more developed the material production, the more advanced the science and technology, the longer distance communication and collaboration, and the more advanced the social form, the more developed the level of information transmission.

The development history of telegraph technology → telephone technology → radio and television technology → wired network technology is the progression of human society's information transmission levels from one-way one-to-one → two-way one-to-one → one-way one-to-many → two-way wired many-to-many. From the 1980s to the present, mobile communication technology has achieved breakthroughs from 1G to 5G, from analog voice to the Internet of Things, realizing two-way wireless many-to-many information transmission. The leap in information transmission density enables media experiences to be upgraded from mobile calls → text messages → online videos → short videos. The decline in information transmission energy consumption has dramatically increased information processing capabilities, with computer processors improving performance by billions of times in just over half a century while reducing power consumption by 90%.[21]

The history of progress in information transmission levels is the history of the progress of information media and media experiences. It has six main dimensions. First, timeliness, addressing the problem of information's timeliness decreasing with increased transmission time. Second, direction, equally important as timeliness, the need for production collaboration and daily life drives media from one-way to two-way and then to multi-directional, the more directions, the higher the efficiency. Third, perception, people can increasingly engage more senses to transmit and receive information, which also means a higher degree of integration of information media, supporting multiple perceptions. Fourth, the convenience of information media is an essential guarantee for information transmission efficiency. The more convenient the media, the easier it is to achieve timely communication and the lower the burden on users. Fifth, agency, with the support of technology, users have increasingly more room to exercise their subjective initiative in the information transmission system, making the presentation of information more diverse and richer in content. Sixth, energy consumption, the unit energy consumption for transmitting equal amounts of information, tends to decrease.

Humanity is approaching a historical milestone where everything is countable and serves as a medium. The vision of the information technology revolution depicted by the concept of the metaverse is precisely the possibility of further changes in the six dimensions of timeliness, direction, perception, convenience, agency, and energy consumption.

First, it is dedicated to achieving real-time feedback with the support of computing networks and digital engines.

Second, it is committed to realizing the interconnection of all things based on high-level interoperability.

Third, it aims to create a high presence and high immersion, realizing a full-sensory experience.

Fourth, it is dedicated to enabling users to travel between physical and digital spaces anytime and anywhere through various terminal forms, realizing convenient transitions.

Fifth, it fully unleashes human agency, liberating creativity and making every user a content producer in the metaverse.

Sixth, it is committed to achieving powerful computing capabilities while significantly reducing unit energy consumption, pursuing a green, low-carbon, and circular development path for the metaverse.

Only by achieving real-time feedback and the interconnection of all things can a full-sensory experience be created. Human understanding and grasp of reality primarily rely on sensory experiences; therefore, a full-sensory experience has already surpassed virtual reality, becoming digital space and digital reality. Digital reality will bring people into a completely new realm of practice, thereby paving the way for the liberation of creativity.

Chapter 3
Industrial Revolution: A Driving Force from the Economic Foundation

The level of scientific and technological progress is a prerequisite for the metaverse, and the imaginations of the metaverse in science fiction novels and movies only appear when related technologies reveal their possibilities in theory or practice. However, science and technology do not evolve independently; their fundamental driving force comes from societal needs, especially those within the economic foundation.

The vitality of the metaverse lies in the objective need to develop modern production methods. Material production has a fundamental impact on social and historical development, and the mode of production occupies a dominant position in all aspects of social life. "The main mode of economic production and exchange in each historical epoch, as well as the social structure necessarily arising from it, is the basis on which the political and spiritual history of that epoch is established, and it is only from this basis that this history can be explained."[22]

Based on the methodology of historical materialism, examining the economic inevitability of the metaverse is fundamentally about whether the metaverse can meet some objective economic development needs or whether the contradictions driving the evolution of the economic foundation will give birth to the metaverse. To explain the evolution of the economic foundation, we must ultimately examine the productive forces and the mode of production. So far, material production has been the absolute prerequisite for the existence and development of human society, and productive forces are the fundamental driving force of historical development. Therefore, this chapter first examines the general laws of the Industrial Revolution; then, based on the objective trends of the new Industrial Revolution, it analyzes the economic inevitability of the metaverse in the field of material production; subsequently, it expands the perspective from the field of material production to the entire economic foundation. Finally, this research tries to answer what other objective conditions need to be met for the great development of the metaverse in conjunction with the history of industrial revolutions.

3.1 General Laws of the Industrial Revolution

The term "Industrial Revolution" is an economic history term. Although industrial technological change is the foundation and essential feature of the Industrial Revolution, the concept of the Industrial Revolution is not limited to the "revolution of industry". Still, it covers a broad transformation and changes in technology, economy, society, and culture during a certain period. Since the 1760s, human society has experienced three industrial revolutions and is currently undergoing the Fourth Industrial Revolution.

Since the First Industrial Revolution, the mode of production for material life has gone through a process of evolution from handicraft production to standardized production, modular production, and intelligent production. The mode of production is based on productive forces, and the level of productive forces is directly reflected in the level of means of production. The development of productive forces and the evolution of the mode of production they drive have enabled enterprises to develop from early synchronous collaboration in the same location to contemporary real-time collaboration in different locations. Currently, corporate networks are the most advanced and representative mode of collaboration. What drives the evolution of the mode of production? From the perspective of productive forces, it is the progress of science and technology. The technological advancements that have driven each Industrial Revolution are chain revolutions triggered by key technological innovations, among which energy technology and communication technology play a dominant role: the former implies an improvement in the level of energy utilization, and the latter implies an improvement in the level of information transmission. Humans can use this to develop and establish new material systems, directly changing the form and scale of collaboration and promoting the innovation of production tools, transportation tools, and communication methods. As Jeremy Rifkin said, the Industrial Revolution was mainly about transforming communication methods and energy systems.[23]

What is the fundamental driving force behind technological

progress? It is a social need. Engels pointed out, "Once society has a technical need, this need is more capable of pushing science forward than ten universities."[24] After the capitalist mode of production emerged, the need to possess surplus value prompted capital to possess, use, and invest in the development of science and technology. Marx said: "Capital does not create science, but it uses science and occupies science for the needs of the production process."[25] Under the socialist system, the social need to develop science and technology is no longer driven by capital accumulation. Still, it is transformed into liberating and developing productive forces to meet the needs of people's aspirations for a better life. Therefore, the governments and state-owned enterprises of socialist countries not only focus on promoting technological progress but also pay more attention to sharing the achievements of technological progress and the development of productive forces with the people.

As mentioned earlier, the metaverse development still requires further revolutions in energy utilization and information transmission levels, which injects strong momentum into the Fourth Industrial Revolution.

3.2 The Metaverse Adapts to the Needs of the Fourth Industrial Revolution

Since the 2008 Global Financial Crisis, the world economy has not yet emerged from stagnation, and developed countries have pinned their hopes of escaping the predicament on the real economy. "Re-industrialization" "Industry 4.0" and "Future Industrial Strategy" have become strategic layouts of developed countries such as the United States, Germany, and Japan. Affected by the COVID-19 pandemic and the international political and economic situation, China's economic growth has slowed down, and the manufacturing industry faces the challenge of transitioning from expanding the incremental market to upgrading the stock market. Using the industrial metaverse to break through the stock market's predicament can help the transformation and upgrading of Chinese manufacturing to intelligent manufacturing. In this context, industry, as the core of the entire material production field, calls for the emergence of the industrial metaverse. The industrial metaverse is the future form of industrial digital transformation and the industrial network.[26]

For the Fourth Industrial Revolution, the social needs of advanced manufacturing are prominently manifested in the following contradictions:

First, the contradiction between demand and design. Due to information asymmetry and information transmission delays, enterprises' perception of demand is not agile enough.

Second, the contradiction between demand and cost. Based on modular and intelligent production, small batches, multiple varieties, and rapid iteration of personalized customization become mainstream, but fixed asset investment associated with machine equipment and production line layout and maintenance becomes a constraint on capital circulation. This forces enterprises to overcome cost issues even if they can perceive demand promptly.

Third, the contradiction between design and manufacturing. Complex industrial products, especially those with complex functions and high application standards, have complicated research, development, testing, and certification processes, inevitably accompanied by high costs and high risks in the transition from design to manufacturing.

Contradictions are the driving force for development. Long-term iterative technological progress in the field of material production, especially in industrial production, has enabled technologies such as cyber-physical systems, 3D designs, extended reality, digital twins, artificial intelligence, the Internet of Things, and cloud computing to form a system and merge into the vision of the industrial metaverse. The industrial metaverse is not only a response to the above contradictions but also a revolution in the mode of production, promoting the liberation and development of social productive forces. Marx pointed out: "The productive forces of society are measured by fixed capital, which exists in the form of objects within fixed capital."[27] Therefore, progress in productive forces will be directly reflected in the material resources that constitute the industrial metaverse, manifested as intelligent systems covering the entire industrial production process, including product design, process development, trial production testing, production line production, equipment debugging, production line inspection, remote maintenance, business management, personnel training, and marketing.[28]

The development of the industrial metaverse will become a powerful tool for addressing these contradictions:

First, strengthening feedback. Establishing real-time feedback communication scenarios between enterprises and users enhances the ability of enterprises to perceive user needs, effectively resolving information asymmetry and transmission delay issues. Enterprises can also let users experience and test products in the metaverse in advance, improving product development based on user feedback.

Second, reducing costs. Using digital twin technology to simulate production layouts, processes, logistics, supply chains, safety assurance, and equipment maintenance improves production planning efficiency, reduces resource consumption, lowers maintenance costs, and supports production safety.[29]

Third, increasing efficiency. The industrial metaverse can help enterprises, developers, and users in different countries and regions within the global production network form efficient collaborations in the digital space, overcoming the negative impact of geographical barriers on collaboration efficiency. The industrial metaverse can perform high-precision simulations and modeling of the entire product development process, conducting experimental verification and product performance testing in a digital environment, improving testing efficiency and reducing the costs associated with testing.

The industrial metaverse is a technological trend presented by the long-term accumulation and evolution of industrial digitization, informatization, intelligentization, and servitization since the 1960s. In this sense, the metaverse represents a tangible technological path and economic trend.

3.3 The Metaverse Will Inevitably Drive the Transformation of the Economic Foundation

The development of the Fourth Industrial Revolution will not only reshape the industry through the industrial metaverse but also reshape the entire economic foundation, from the underlying material production field to the financial system. This transformation of the economic foundation is an inevitable trend: first, the transformation of the material production field will inevitably promote the evolution of the economic foundation by driving changes in production relations and exchange relations; second, production development meets demand and continuously creates new demands, which in turn stimulate production development and drive the evolution of the economic foundation. From a technical and economic perspective, the systemic transformation of the economic foundation by the metaverse will realize the distribution of productive forces according to computing power networks and the digitization of the total social production process.

3.3.1 Productive Forces Distributed by Computing Power Networks

In the digital economy era, computing power is a productive force. The new round of technological revolution and the Fourth Industrial Revolution characterized by intelligentization are pushing humanity into an era of intelligent interconnection. On the one hand, the traditional two-tier model of data centers and terminals cannot meet the demands of specific application scenarios such as the Internet of Things, vehicle networking, and industrial Internet for data center network throughput, concurrent computing, and storage. On the other hand, developing new technologies such as 5G has generated massive data at the network edge, thereby promoting the diffusion of computing power from a few data centers to the application side.[30] At the same time, intelligentization endows application-side terminal machines with more functions, higher efficiency, and faster response speeds. This makes computing power a core technological component of productive forces in the digital economy era—the extent of the computing power network determines the range of collaboration expansion and the scope of enterprises' optimization of factor allocation.

The computing power network will change the distribution pattern of productivity, giving rise to decentralized production, achieving a state where "computing power is available, production can occur", For most capital-intensive industries (such as metallurgy, petroleum, and machinery manufacturing) and technology-intensive industries (such as machine tool and robotics industries), their technical characteristics determine that centralized production is not easily replaceable, but the computing power network can make them more flexible and agile. For some products and services whose production is relatively easier (such as manufacturing through 3D printing), the computing power network can potentially support the decentralized production of these products: the research and design phase relies on the computing power network for self-service and intelligentization, while the manufacturing phase can be distributed like ATMs, even entering ordinary households. The computing power network can enable real-time design, production, and delivery of digital products based on bitstreams.

3.3.2 Digitalization of the Social Production Process

Social production includes four stages: production, consumption, distribution, and exchange (circulation). These four stages are not separate domains but are organically unified in the social production process. Various industries and business models exist and develop based on different stages of the social production process.

As a technology, industry, and ecology aggregator, the development of the metaverse will inevitably drive many emerging industries and promote new business models in existing industries, realizing the digitalization of the social production process.

The deepening of digitalization in the social production process will strengthen the integration of production, consumption, distribution, and exchange. For example, the dispersion and sinking of productivity with the computing power network can make the production end more sensitive to the feedback information of digital products in consumption and circulation. It can also enable ordinary consumers to actively organize the production of personalized products using the computing power network, achieving real-time design, production, delivery, consumption, and feedback.

Digitalizing the social production process will inevitably promote the development of digital currencies and digital assets, leading to new production methods and business models. Currently, the currency transformation based on blockchain technology has become an irreversible trend. The development of sovereign digital currencies, established on a multi-center architecture based on distributed ledgers,[31] will become the lifeblood of the metaverse economic system. People's digital products created in the metaverse relying on their intelligence and creativity can obtain unique digital certificates once generated, having asset attributes.[32] Their production and circulation can bring economic value, incentivize users, and form the growth momentum of the metaverse economic system. Based on blockchain technology, distributed digital identities can integrate digital avatars in different metaverse application scenarios and combined with identity traceability, protect the intellectual property rights of real-world creators and form business models based on digital assets. The two-way circulation of digital and real assets will also create new currency circulation mechanisms and new business models.

3.3.3 New Economic Systems and Economic Laws

The metaverse economic system is based on blockchain technology, representing a technological leap compared to the Internet's TCP/IP protocol. On the one hand, the Internet's underlying protocol cannot effectively guarantee information security and requires protective measures like firewalls. On the other hand, the Internet operates based on simple underlying protocols and a wealth of application layer protocols, which demand high technical skills from developers. This inevitably gives rise to platform oligopolies and monopolies on data and privacy.[33] Blockchain technology lowers the entry barrier for ordinary people, holding the potential to help dissolve platform and data monopolies.

The metaverse economic system will inevitably form new economic laws and institutions. Economic laws are historical, and economic institutions are generated. Firstly, as people access the metaverse with digital identities, their digital production and consumption can, to some extent, be separated from real-world production, inevitably forming different laws and driving the evolution of economic systems. Secondly, technologies like digital twins and augmented reality will improve collaboration efficiency, promoting a flattening of collaborative and production organizational forms. Blockchain and other technologies may drive the evolution of production organizational forms at the underlying logic level. Thirdly, economic activities in the metaverse are built based on information transmission at the speed of light, enabling simultaneous production, distribution, sales, and allocation. Fourthly, with the trend of robots replacing a large portion of the labor force, the metaverse economic system can create new jobs and social roles. If effective measures to control monopolies and establish new distribution systems are in place, it is possible to achieve economic development and human liberation through more liberated creative activities, paving the way for the all-round development of humanity.

3.3.4 Exploring New Dimensions of Economic Development

Time compression and spatial expansion are two fundamental dimensions of economic development. Time compression is achieved through the development of productive forces and changes in production relations, enhancing collaboration efficiency, improving labor tools, accelerating information transmission, and improving labor objects (such as scientific breeding). Spatial expansion is realized through geographical expansion, such as colonial expansion, commodity exports, capital exports, the development of marine, aviation and aerospace economies, and the transformation of existing spaces, such as the reconstruction of urban above-ground and underground spaces and the creation of urban landscapes.

The metaverse can bring stronger time compression and spatial expansion to economic development. Firstly, the metaverse can create remote synchronous collaboration scenarios, greatly improving the efficiency of global production networks. Secondly, people can establish a unified digital identity in different metaverse application scenarios, allowing multiple digital avatars to operate in parallel within their respective metaverse dimensions, creating a time multiplication effect. Thirdly, the "physical rules" within specific metaverse application scenarios differ from those in physical reality. While the "physical rules" of digital reality can be defined, those of physical reality can only be discovered and adhered to. Therefore, the metaverse's time and space are not only theoretically infinite but can also transcend the physical rules of the real world to some extent, allowing people's imagination and creativity to be fully unleashed within the metaverse.

3.4 The Prospect of the Metaverse Seen From the "Tool Machine Revolution"

Why does the metaverse seem to have a promising future, yet we have yet to see disruptive metaverse products? We are currently in the early stages of a new technological revolution represented by the metaverse, and to fully stimulate and release the potential of the metaverse's technological revolution, we need to find the metaverse's "tool machine revolution". As Zhao Xing et al have pointed out, we are still in the "pre-metaverse era", with varying technological paths, scarce application scenarios, and unclear governance paths.[34]

Marx believed that the starting point of the First Industrial Revolution was not the power revolution (Watt's improved steam engine) but the tool machine revolution (the spinning jenny): "All developed machines consist of three essentially different parts: the engine, the transmission mechanism, the tool machine or working machine.... The tool machine is the starting point of the 18th-century Industrial Revolution."[35] The steam engine invented at the end of the 17th century did not cause the Industrial Revolution because the direct effect on the labor object was the craftsman's hands and feet, and "the number of natural production tools limits the number of tools that a person can use simultaneously, that is, the number of organs of their own body."[36] In other words, the power advances at the end of the 17th century lacked application scenarios that could fully release their energy. The craftsman's physiological conditions limited the upper limit in manual production.

The purpose of inventing the spinning jenny was to overcome the physiological limitations of manual labor. Once an automatic working tool machine was born, the contradiction within productivity transformed: the object of power supply changed from human to machine, and the power supply had to adapt to the high-speed uniform movement of spinning machinery, while human, animal, water, and wind power could not meet this need. The contradiction between the newly born tool machine and the old steam engine prompted Watt to invent the double-acting steam engine.[37] Marx pointed out: "Only when the labor object passes successively through a series of interconnected different stages of the process, and these processes are completed by a series of different and complementary tool machines, the real machine system replaces the individual machines."[38] Economist W. W. Rostow noted that the Industrial Revolution enabled "British inventors and innovators to finally solve the problem of using cotton thread as the warp, thus competing with the nimble hands of Indians using machines."[39] The machine system driven by natural energy replaced physical labor, leading to a historic transition from an agricultural society to an industrial society.[40]

The tool machine revolution and the power revolution together constitute the two legs of the First Industrial Revolution. This historical fact shows that the release of the power revolution and its revolutionary energy depends on the practical needs of application scenarios.

As mentioned in the previous chapter, computing power is the driving force behind the metaverse. This power system includes various forms such as cloud computing, edge computing, terminal computing, and spatial computing. Currently, there is still a long way to go for computing power to support the mature form of the metaverse and to overcome the hard constraints of Moore's Law (that computational progress will become significantly faster, smaller, and more efficient over time) slowing down. More importantly, various application scenarios within the metaverse are still brewing. There is no shortage of demand from segmented application scenarios for the producer metaverse oriented toward enterprise users (especially the industrial metaverse), but the metaverse oriented toward ordinary consumers still lacks disruptive products that can change people's lifestyles and ways of interacting. It can be imagined that the current level of computing power systems may be similar to the steam power systems at the end of the 17th century. On the one hand, we still need a "tool machine revolution" in various segmented application scenarios of the metaverse. Only when these "tool machine revolutions" demonstrate their superiority in market competition and user choice will the power revolution (computing power revolution) be fully stimulated; on the other hand, we also need progress in industrial production (especially chip production) itself to support breakthroughs in computing power technology from both hardware and software perspectives.

Chapter 4
Value Philosophy:
Pursuing Free and Comprehensive Development

The value norms of the metaverse answer the value judgment question of what the metaverse "should be". Advances in science and technology and social and economic development should promote human liberation, not become tools to dominate people; they should promote improving social civilization levels rather than fostering social ills. Currently, the understanding of the metaverse in domestic business and theoretical circles mainly focuses on "objects", defining or explaining the metaverse from the perspective of technical composition, technology trends, or economic characteristics.[41] Any technology is born for specific needs and purposes, so understanding the metaverse should include the factual judgment of "what it is" and the value judgment of "what it should be". In other words, in the context of the unfulfilled human destiny community, what the metaverse "should be" is a more strategic and global dimension.

4.1 The Metaverse Reflects Humanity's Pursuit of Free and Comprehensive Development

The metaverse is a new field of human civilization and a milestone for humanity's journey toward free and comprehensive development. Natural people in physical space are digitized into digital humans in the metaverse. Digital humans become the active subjects of metaverse civilization. From the perspective of metaverse civilization and metaverse society, digital humans are also digital citizens within the metaverse.

From the perspective of human life, the primitive impulse to break free from the inherent limitations of natural laws and physiological conditions in the natural world is the "gene" of human civilization's evolution. From the perspective of human civilization, the spiral ascending process of civilization's evolution constantly realizes a higher degree of freedom and liberation for humans.

The greatness of human life lies in breaking the inherent "impossibilities" in nature and, through practice, humanizing nature to strengthen and expand our own abilities. The use of stone tools in early human civilizations embodies the infinite possibilities of using tools to extend our minds and limbs. Ships and submarines enable humans to overcome the limitations of water on the human body, airplanes and airships allow humans to break the limitations of flight, and letters, telegrams, radio, landline telephones, television, mobile phones, and the Internet enable humans to break the time and space limitations of information transmission. American statesman Alexander Hamilton once said, "The use of machinery has a very important role in the total industry of a nation. It is an artificial force used to support man's natural force and is an extension of limbs and an increase in power for all purposes of labor."[42]

The metaverse can achieve leaps in perceptual abilities. By accessing the metaverse through convenient terminals, humans can obtain more powerful visual, auditory, and tactile senses and, through technologies such as brain-computer interfaces and eye-tracking, unprecedentedly endow the perceptual system with the ability to actively output. In other words, the metaverse can achieve perception as action, and input as output.

The metaverse can bring about a qualitative change in life forms. The significance of the metaverse goes far beyond replacing and extending human minds and limbs like ordinary tools and machines. Instead, silicon-based technology empowers carbon-based life forms, enabling carbon-based life to enter the silicon-based digital spacetime. When the metaverse covers all aspects of social production and life, silicon-based terminal devices and interfaces will become essential to people's lives, even becoming a part of the human body. The fusion of carbon-based and silicon-based life forms is the direction of evolution for life forms in the information society.

The metaverse can help life traverse time and space. A person's physical self can be projected into multiple metaverse application scenarios, expanding their practical abilities and boundaries through digital avatars. In each application scenario, unique spacetime experiences can be had, effectively and greatly extending human life. The development of economic systems and the progress of social civilization since the Industrial Revolution largely stem from the increase in average life expectancy. With a longer life expectancy, people can better learn knowledge, produce knowledge, and realize intergenerational knowledge transfer.

The metaverse can reshape lifestyles, ways of interaction, and social relationships. The expansion of human life in the metaverse will inevitably shape new lifestyles and ways of interaction. Digital life and digital interactions based on digital identities will form unprecedented social life scenarios, changing people in physical reality. Marx pointed out that the essence of man is "the sum of all social relations".[43] When traditional face-to-face interactions evolve into network interactions and, in the future, into interactions between digital humans in digital reality, not only will people in the metaverse inevitably form social relationships different from those in physical reality, but these relationships will also shape social interactions and social relationships in physical reality, thereby changing people's thoughts, ideas, and behaviors.

4.2 Strategic and Global Nature of Value Normativity Issues in the Metaverse

The free and comprehensive development of the metaverse will not be naturally realized, so the issue of value normativity is raised.

First, from the perspective of technological advancement, the path of technological progress is neither unique nor predetermined. Factors such as market competition, government intervention, capital monopoly, and national competition can all influence the technological path. This means that we must consider the value dimension of the metaverse in advance to guide the evolution of the metaverse's technological system with the common values of all humankind, preventing the metaverse from becoming a tool for tech giants to seek market share or monopoly profits. The following are important factors that may affect the technological path of the metaverse:

The complexity of user needs. If technological innovation disregards ethical values and one-sidedly meets users' distorted or even extreme needs, it may lead to chaotic and disordered development of the metaverse civilization or even turn it into a haven and breeding ground for falsehood, evil, and ugliness.

The possibility of user addiction. Is the metaverse intended to enhance people's abilities to understand better and change the world, or will it lead to immersion and addiction in digital spacetime? If the technological path competition does not receive guidance from ethical values, some companies will inevitably try to exploit the potential addictiveness of the metaverse to captivate users.

The purpose of technological innovation. The purpose of the entities driving technological innovation is an important determinant of the technological path. Will the metaverse become a tool monopolized by a few large companies to obtain monopoly profits or a tool controlled by individual countries to achieve hegemony, or should it benefit the entire society and all of humanity? Different purposes will inevitably stimulate the technological system to evolve in different directions.

Second, social existence determines social consciousness, and practical activities determine thoughts and ideas. People's activities in the metaverse and experiences will inevitably change their concepts and cognition. If the metaverse lacks ethical, moral, and legal order, it is highly likely that users will lose themselves in the metaverse and even turn to pornography, violence, and extremism.

Third, the metaverse can establish multiple digital realities intertwined with physical reality, providing real-time feedback and immersive experiences and allowing people's physical selves to be projected into digital reality and engage in activities as digital humans. This means that the ethical, moral, and legal issues that exist in physical reality also exist in the metaverse. Without regulation, the metaverse's development will inevitably lead to numerous ethical issues and even violent conflicts.

Fourth, traditional media and the Internet have historically been arenas for Western countries to assert their discursive and cultural hegemony. The vast majority of the world's population in developing countries have no control and are even infiltrated and incited by "color revolutions" due to their inability to dominate public opinion. Therefore, the construction of the metaverse's digital spacetime must adhere to a civilized and orderly metaverse governance perspective and insist on the fundamental concern of the common values of all humankind.

Fifth, foreign giant monopoly companies such as Google and Apple have already begun to lay out the metaverse and engage in competition. Behind these giant monopoly companies is the support of Western governments. If the control and influence over technological standards, underlying protocols, and the establishment

of basic order are lost, it will inevitably lead to developing countries, including China, continuing to be in a passive position regarding discourse, public opinion, and culture in the metaverse.

4.3 The Metaverse as a Response to the Shared Future for Mankind Through a Technological Revolution

The value dimension of the metaverse fundamentally answers the question of whom the metaverse should serve. The metaverse should serve the common values of all humanity, not the profits of a few tech giants; it should serve a harmonious social and civilizational ecosystem, not the unbridled release of desires; it should serve the journey toward the stars and the ocean, not as a veil to cover up social contradictions; it should serve the mutual benefit of all countries in the world, not as a space for a few countries to operate hegemony. Past technological revolutions have built material foundations for liberating and developing productive forces, changing human lifestyles, expanding human living spaces, and promoting political and social civilization progress, but they have also been accompanied by colonization, exploitation, monopoly, wars, financial predation, social divisions, political polarization, cultural invasion, and ecological disasters. These issues continue to plague human society, and some are even intensifying. Should the metaverse, which depicts the prospect of a new round of technological revolution, make a difference in alleviating or even solving these problems and avoiding new ones? The answer is obviously yes.

The metaverse should be a ladder toward a community with a shared future for mankind and a digital spacetime for realizing the common values of all humanity. To actively guide the metaverse to serve the common values of all humanity, we should adhere to the principles and propositions contained in the concept of a community of shared future in cyberspace, such as development, security, governance, and inclusiveness[44], and follow a path of harmonious, innovative, green, secure, and win-win industrial development.

Harmony. The metaverse should form equal social relationships, a good civilizational ecology, and orderly digital spaces. The metaverse is a domain of advanced human civilization, not a place for conflict, violence, or crime.

Innovation. Innovation is the theme of economic activities in the metaverse and the manifestation of the metaverse promoting individuals' free and comprehensive development. The digital content created by people in the metaverse is the source of its vitality.

Green. The development of metaverse civilization depends on external environments, especially ecological support. The metaverse development should adhere to green, low-carbon, and circular principles, achieving green collaboration across the entire industry in core system construction and interactive system development.

Security. Security is a fundamental need for individuals and society. The metaverse should achieve unified privacy, data, and national security at the user, platform, and national levels.

Win-win. Industrial development must pay attention to the pattern of interests, and a win-win situation directly reflects the metaverse industry serving the human destiny community. Win-win for platforms and users, within and between countries, is the inherent requirement of the metaverse industry and civilization.

Chapter 5
Civilized and Orderly:
China's Solution for Metaverse Governance

The direction and path of technological progress are not predetermined but are shaped by various factors such as existing technology, market competition, state intervention, ethics, and legal systems. Science and technology will not naturally lead to goodness and well-being; technology can be used for good by guiding and regulating them. The future metaverse will either serve the people or succumb to interest groups, either serve the common values of all humanity or succumb to the hegemony of Western countries, and either immerse people in exquisite illusions or propel humanity toward the stars and oceans. Where should we go? It depends on human action.

The development of the metaverse cannot be separated from its governance. Governance inherently has a public nature. When considering governance issues, both the design of the system and the outcomes it produces should focus on the public interest.

Currently, the United States hopes to maintain its global leadership in cyberspace governance and extend it to metaverse governance, while foreign tech monopolies rely on market competition to influence and control the discourse on metaverse governance. Developing countries, represented by China, with strong metaverse growth potential, should and must propose a metaverse governance solution that transcends national and capitalist hegemony, effectively safeguarding the rights and interests of the vast majority of developing countries with relatively backward technology. As a new domain of human civilization, the metaverse should and must form a new frontier of human civilization beyond zero-sum games and capital logic, advancing toward individuals' free and comprehensive development.

The foundation of metaverse governance is respecting digital sovereignty, the direction is the community of human destiny, the guide is the common values of all humanity, the principle is civilized and orderly, and the path promotes multilateral co-governance to achieve joint construction and win-win outcomes.

5.1 Governance Challenges in Building a Civilized Metaverse

The metaverse will inevitably have externalities, i.e., it will inevitably impact physical reality (side effects). As General Secretary Xi Jinping pointed out: "Technology is a weapon for development, but it can also be a source of risk."[45] How to properly address the externalities inherent in the metaverse is an important issue that cannot be avoided and should be addressed before the commercialization of the metaverse. These externalities mainly manifest as the following governance challenges:

Cognitive barriers challenge. On the one hand, the full-sensory experience in the metaverse and the existence and activities of digital humans will have an impact on people's cognitive patterns, forcing them to face questions like "Who are they?" and "Do they belong to humanity?" On the other hand, human cognition is built on sensory experiences. The full-sensory experience in the digital reality may cause people to lose themselves in the metaverse, unable to effectively distinguish it from the external environment

(the real world). Therefore, at the beginning of building a metaverse civilization, the identity of digital humans and the priority of the metaverse versus the real world must be considered.

Ethical and moral challenges. A distinct ethical and moral system will inevitably emerge in the metaverse civilization, and the activities of digital humans will undoubtedly challenge existing ethical and moral systems. The metaverse breaks through human's inherent limitations in time, space, and physiology, enriching human existence, enhancing human capabilities, expanding human activities, and meeting human needs, reshaping ethics and morals from the bottom up.

Challenges of defining rights and responsibilities. There are two basic categories of digital humans in the metaverse: those with corresponding physical entities in the real world and those who are purely virtual without any physical counterparts. When digital humans interact in the metaverse, issues of rights, obligations, and responsibilities arise, and conflicts between digital humans. To address this challenge, it is necessary to define digital citizens and clarify their rights and responsibilities based on their categories, ensuring that digital human behavior is accountable and traceable.

Civilizational conflict challenges. Collisions between heterogeneous civilizations and cultures in the metaverse will inevitably be more direct and intense than in the internet era. When people with opposing economic interests, political views, and religious beliefs in the physical world encounter each other in the metaverse, the immersive full-sensory experience will have a much stronger impact than the internet. To resolve these conflicts, a community with a shared future for mankind must be built in the physical world. To make the metaverse a precursor to a community with a shared future for mankind, a fair metaverse social system must be established rather than simply replicating existing social structures.

Technological monopoly challenges. Western developed countries and international monopoly capitals will undoubtedly seek to extend their technological monopoly status into the future metaverse civilization, thus achieving governance hegemony and appropriating surplus value in the metaverse. Technological monopoly is fundamentally at odds with a community with a shared future for mankind. Therefore, a more equitable and rational international technological standard governance system should be promoted in the metaverse to ensure that it serves all users equally.

Digital currency challenges. The metaverse has an economic system that interacts with the physical world, with a payment and settlement system that matches this economy. Currently, non-fungible tokens (NFTs) have gained a user base due to their frictionless cross-border fund transfers, even beginning to erode traditional sovereign currencies. If platform companies with technological advantages dominate financial activities in the metaverse, traditional financial regulation will face challenges.[46] If the world fails to establish unified regulations, cross-border arbitrage and money laundering crimes will inevitably emerge. If the United States leverages its traditional network hegemony to build digital currency dominance, it will threaten the national interests of many developing countries.

Digital sovereignty challenges. General Secretary Xi Jinping pointed out that the new round of technological and industrial revolutions represented by information technology has injected strong momentum into economic and social development while bringing many new challenges to countries' sovereignty, security, and development interests worldwide.[47] Respecting each other's sovereignty is a basic requirement of the global governance system and essential for metaverse civilization. Digital reality will not be entirely separate from physical reality, so that sovereign nations will have digital sovereignty demands in the metaverse. A metaverse pursuing a shared human destiny should respect digital sovereignty as a prerequisite and avoid repeating existing hegemony issues in metaverse civilization.

Content security challenges. Hegemonic countries, extremists, and malicious forces will inevitably try to use the high immersion of the metaverse to spread harmful information. The metaverse's economic system may also bring about issues such as money laundering, tax base erosion, and profit shifting. The high real-time nature of the metaverse poses significant challenges to content security regulation. These issues require a coordinated solution through top-level design and technical infrastructure.

5.2 Toward a Metaverse Community of Shared Future with an Orderly and Civilized Metaverse

The metaverse is a new domain for human civilization and

will inevitably reshape human civilization. Who leads metaverse governance and what values it upholds are crucial for the future of human civilization. General Secretary Xi Jinping pointed out: "Cyberspace is a common activity space for humanity, and the future of cyberspace should be jointly controlled by countries worldwide. Countries should strengthen communication, expand consensus, deepen cooperation, and jointly build a community of shared future in cyberspace."[48]

Shared values of all humanity are the meta-values of metaverse civilization. Meta-values reflect the essence and core of values. By upholding shared values for all humanity, we can work together to build a community of shared future in cyberspace, promote its development toward a metaverse community of shared future, and make the metaverse a forerunner of a community with a shared future for mankind.

Whenever human civilization reaches a critical juncture, advanced ideas and values are needed to guide its direction. On September 28, 2015, General Secretary Xi Jinping delivered a keynote speech at the 70th session of the United Nations General Assembly, stating, "Peace, development, fairness, justice, democracy, and freedom are the common values of all humanity."[49] The common values of all humanity look at the future of humanity from a holistic perspective, advocating the formation of the greatest common denominator of values based on mutual respect, seeking common ground while preserving differences, and learning from each other's civilizations. This is done to build a consensus on the values of a community with a shared future for mankind and to achieve joint advancement in development, joint maintenance of security, joint participation in governance, and shared benefits from achievements.[50]

The governance of a civilized and orderly metaverse entails the following connotations:

Respect digital sovereignty and oppose hegemony. A nation's government is the core actor in promoting social development and maintaining social order. Respecting national sovereignty is a basic principle of international relations. National sovereignty has historical boundaries, and when human society expands its living space to the internet, it gives rise to cyberspace sovereignty. As the internet evolves into the metaverse, cyberspace sovereignty will inevitably be upgraded to digital sovereignty. The construction and development of the metaverse should change the old order of Western countries, putting hegemony above sovereignty and establishing a new order of metaverse civilization that respects digital sovereignty and the differences between countries.

Promote fairness and justice, transcend digital monopoly. Fairness and justice have long been the common pursuit of all humanity. The persistent issues of monopoly, infringement, and tax avoidance by technology giants and big capital in cyberspace are obstacles to fairness and justice and have been questioned and criticized by people worldwide. Metaverse governance must establish a governance system that transcends capital logic and digital monopoly. The governance of metaverse technology standards should avoid the issues of a few technology giants exploiting monopoly profits through controlling standard alliances, standard essential patents, and patent pools.

Advocate for multi-centrism and be cautious about decentralization. The decentralization features of some underlying metaverse technologies, such as blockchain, do not equate to decentralized governance. Technically, the construction of the metaverse must meet requirements such, as permission, authentication, compatibility, and interconnectivity, which inherently indicate the necessity and feasibility of external regulation. From a governance perspective, authority and governance centers are inevitable in human society: "Without authority, there can be no consistent action."[51] Therefore, centralization does not mean backwardness, and decentralization does not imply advancement. The idea of decentralized governance is, to some extent, a normative claim and does not represent an actual trend. In fact, decentralized governance is likely to benefit monopolistic capital and hegemonic countries. To serve the interests of the vast majority of people worldwide, we should promote multi-centric governance based on respect for digital sovereignty.

Advocate for equality and respect and maintain a common life. People's sense of gain, happiness, and security are the primary criteria for measuring the welfare of the metaverse. On the one hand, these feelings come from the satisfaction of diverse needs, so metaverse governance must treat the diversity of human needs with an attitude of equality and respect. By strengthening infrastructure construction, we can popularize the metaverse in relatively underdeveloped countries and regions and achieve equal access to the metaverse. On the other hand, individual freedom is bound by the freedom of others, so metaverse governance cannot take a laissez-faire attitude toward needs. The satisfaction of diverse needs must be based on maintaining a common life.

Discern the relationship between the digital and physical worlds and establish a good order. The metaverse originates from and is based on real society; without the external environment provided by real society, the metaverse has no starting point. Therefore, we must discern the priority between digital reality and physical reality, ensuring that any ethics, morals, or laws within the metaverse do not violate the bottom line of physical reality and prevent the metaverse from becoming a lawless zone. Like real society, the metaverse should respect freedom and protect order. Freedom is the purpose of order, and order guarantees freedom. We need to clarify the ethical and legal relationship between natural persons in physical reality and their digital avatars in different types of the metaverse. We should develop behavioral guidelines for digital personas based on the varying immersion and realism levels in specific application scenarios.

Ensure digital security and share development achievements.

While the metaverse brings wonderful experiences to human life and new momentum for economic development, it will inevitably be accompanied by new digital security challenges. The high level of digital-physical integration and human-machine integration in the metaverse imposes higher demands on digital security. Building a robust digital security barrier for the metaverse can only be achieved after a period of time; and it requires concerted efforts from countries worldwide. We must strengthen the top-level design and improve institutional rules, standard systems, and supporting policies to ensure digital security for all humanity to share the fruits of development.

Coordinate the entire industry chain and adhere to green development. Environmental and energy issues are significant challenges humanity faces, and overcoming environmental and energy thresholds is crucial for the metaverse. Although the emissions and energy consumption per unit of information transmitted by humans have significantly decreased over the past two centuries, the explosive growth of total information has led to a considerable increase in overall emissions and energy consumption. We should coordinate green development across the

entire metaverse industry chain, promoting humanity's transition to a green information civilization through technological progress and scientific governance.

To jointly build metaverse governance, share metaverse civilization, and move toward a metaverse community of shared future, we should value the principles of first-setting issues and first-establishing rules, avoiding passively following the agenda and rules set by monopolistic.

5.3 Policy Principles for Metaverse Governance in the New Era

While promoting metaverse governance to realize the common values of all humanity, we also need to actively explore and plan our country's metaverse governance, establish the political requirements for the party to govern the metaverse, and evolve from a comprehensive network governance system to a comprehensive metaverse governance system. By building a metaverse rule of law and creating a clear digital space in the metaverse, the success of the new era metaverse governance system based on socialism as the fundamental principle will demonstrate Chinese wisdom in metaverse governance to the world and lead civilized and orderly global metaverse governance.

This research attempts to propose the following policy principles for new era metaverse governance:

Uphold the principle of putting people first. People-centeredness is an essential attribute of Marxism.[52] The metaverse's construction, development, and governance are ultimately for the people. Respect the wisdom, creativity, and achievements of the masses, build a metaverse that people can participate in, identify with, and share, and avoid erroneous directions or one-sided views prioritizing capital, entertainment, or technology.

Persist in advancing both practical exploration and theoretical innovation. Practice is the source of theory, the fundamental driving force for theory development, and the only criterion for testing truth. Theory, in turn, actively influences practice, and scientific theory can guide practice. In the early stages of metaverse development, we should encourage innovation and development in practice and actively innovate in theory to form a good situation where practice and theory complement each other.

Insist on the synergy between top-level design and technical foundation. In the early stages of metaverse development, we should plan early for the regulation of the underlying architecture, guide the metaverse governance system through top-level design, consolidate the responsibility of metaverse platform entities, and clarify user responsibilities to avoid responsibility vacuums.

Adhere to properly handling the relationship between the government and the market. In the early stages of metaverse development, we should manage the relationship between the government and the market, avoid the absence of regulation and law at the beginning of new industries and new formats, and establish a standardized market order while fully releasing the market vitality of the metaverse industry, and play a centralized, unified, efficient, and authoritative role in governance based on adhering to the overall national security concept and balancing the dual goals of coordinated development and security.

Persist in the integration of the digital economy and the real economy. The report of the 20th Party Congress emphasizes that we must continue to focus on the real economy in pursuing economic growth, accelerate the development of the digital economy, further integrate it with the real economy, and build internationally competitive digital industry clusters.[53] The metaverse is an important direction for the development of the digital economy and a crucial force for promoting the transformation and upgrading of the real economy under the background of a new round of technological revolution. We must seize the key opportunity for the integrated development of the digital economy and the real economy.

Uphold the coordination between industrial growth and technology leadership. The discourse and leadership in global metaverse governance require both strong industrial scale support and a solid technological standard leading position. Therefore, to achieve a leading position, we must achieve the synergy between industrial ecosystem cultivation and core technology research and development, especially in the underlying core technology research and development and the underlying architecture design standards. In the early stages of metaverse development, we should focus on independent innovation and control, strengthen the national strategic technological force in the metaverse industry, fully use the advantages of a new national system and large-scale market, and avoid dependence on core technologies.

Insist on balancing the guidance of social norms and legal regulation. The real-time nature of user behavior and content production in the metaverse poses technical challenges for content security and supervision. As a digital reality space, its basic governance mechanisms can be connected and referred to as physical reality, forming a governance system that runs through external, ex-ante, and ex-post aspects:

First, improve the literacy of metaverse users through education and guidance in physical reality;

Second, guide user behavior norms in the metaverse, enabling digital individuals to develop a sense of order;

Third, develop and improve the legal system regarding the metaverse and govern disorderly phenomena according to law;

Fourth, establish and improve the public safety system in the metaverse, addressing the challenges high immersion and real-time aspects pose to public safety in the metaverse, ensuring digital citizens have public safety protection like citizens in physical reality.

Insist on coordinating open development and security

maintenance. The metaverse must follow the path of open development. The metaverse's openness, real-time, and immersive nature will inevitably profoundly change the media, scenarios, and content that carry the value system, posing higher requirements for metaverse security governance. We should promote forming a metaverse governance system that unifies proactive guidance, preventive measures, security supervision, and emergency response, with unified governance mechanisms and effectiveness.

5.4 Building a Metaverse Civilization Ecosystem

General Secretary Xi Jinping emphasized at the first China Internet Civilization Conference that the construction of internet civilization should "persist in the unity of development and governance, the integration of online and off-line, and widely converge the forces of goodness and progress". Based on adhering to the "Four Principles" and "Five Proposals" of global internet governance, we should construct a metaverse civilization ecosystem guided by the common values of all humanity.

The "Four Principles" of global internet governance are:

(1) Respect for cyber sovereignty, applying the principles and spirit of the United Nations Charter to cyberspace;

(2) Maintaining peace and security, recognizing the significance of a stable and prosperous cyberspace for the world;

(3) Promote openness and cooperation, embracing the concepts of mutual trust, mutual benefit, and rejecting zero-sum games and winner-takes-all approaches;

(4) Build a well-ordered cyberspace, advocating for both freedom and order.

The "Five Proposals" for global internet governance are:

(1) Accelerate the construction of global internet infrastructure and promote interconnectivity;

(2) Create a platform for online cultural exchange and sharing, promoting mutual learning and communication;

(3) Encourage innovation in the digital economy and promote shared prosperity;

(4) Ensure cybersecurity and foster orderly development;

(5) Construct an internet governance system that promotes fairness and justice.

The metaverse civilization ecosystem should adhere to the unity of prevention and punishment, and the unity of moral guidance, legal regulation, and technological guarantees, specifically including five dimensions: platform construction, application development, community rules, economic system, and digital citizens:

Improve platform construction. Focus on metaverse governance based on platforms and improve metaverse platform construction from the underlying logic of metaverse platforms.

Regulate application development. Strengthen supervision and guidance in metaverse application development to reduce and avoid applications that exploit policy and legal loopholes and damage the metaverse civilization ecology and governance.

Guide community self-governance. Communities are the basic units of social governance and will inevitably be the basic units of metaverse governance. By guiding community self-governance, fully mobilize the sense of participation, responsibility, and mission of digital citizens.

Innovate economic systems. Actively develop sovereign digital currencies, explore new monetary circulation laws and economic operation laws, strengthen digital asset protection, and positively interact with the economic systems in physical space-time.

Shape digital citizens. Enable digital individuals in the metaverse to participate in constructing a common life as digital citizens. Advocate for digital citizens to consciously abide by morality and law, establish equal social and economic relationships and build a good civilization ecology and orderly digital space.

Chapter 6
Conclusion

At the Commemoration of the 200th Anniversary of Marx's Birth, General Secretary Xi Jinping emphasized: "To win advantages, take the initiative, and win the future, we must constantly improve our ability to analyze and solve practical problems with Marxism."[54]

This study focuses on the metatheory level, seeking the fundamental nature of the metaverse. Based on metatheory research, we attempt to construct a "China Independent Knowledge System" about the metaverse, making theoretical explorations to secure discourse power, leadership, agenda-setting power, and rule-making power for China and other developing countries in global metaverse governance.

6.1 Understanding the Concept of the Metaverse

There are various interpretations of the concept of the metaverse in society. Without first clarifying this issue, it is difficult to avoid excessive optimism or skepticism about the metaverse. This study uses dialectical materialism and historical materialism as its methodology, examining the historical inevitability and objective reality of the metaverse from the perspective of scientific and technological progress and the evolution of economic foundations. The metaverse is defined from three perspectives:

First, the metaverse is a technological, industrial, and ecological aggregate.

Second, the metaverse aggregates the vision of the information technology revolution.

Third, the metaverse is a system of intelligent interconnection of all things, integrating humans, machines, and objects.

The above three perspectives all emphasize the integrative nature of the metaverse concept:

The metaverse is not a specific technology but rather an integration of multiple technological systems. This requires thinking about and planning the metaverse with a holistic mindset and strategic vision. However, it is also essential to realize that many specific goals of the metaverse currently need to be attainable or clarified due to existing technological limitations.

As a complex system, the metaverse is ultimately composed of numerous subsystems, and its final form and appearance will gradually emerge during development. Therefore, it is crucial to pay attention to the layout of various specific technologies and applications, especially core technologies and critical systems involving the underlying logic of the metaverse. Developing the metaverse relies not only on strategic planning but also on concrete technologies and applications. We need to focus on the overall picture while also addressing implementation issues. The importance of implementation is evident in how ChatGPT has overshadowed the metaverse. In contrast to the metaverse's integrative or comprehensive nature, ChatGPT addresses more specific problems, and despite its limitations, it is ultimately easier to implement. This may be a significant factor in ChatGPT's recent surpassing of the metaverse department within Microsoft. This does not mean that the metaverse is unreliable but rather serves as

a reminder that "a great tree grows from a tiny sprout; a nine-story tower begins with a mound of earth". Various sub-technologies supporting the metaverse will undoubtedly emerge before the metaverse itself. Long-term accumulation of technological research and development and market expansion must be emphasized. Whether we can grasp discourse power and leadership in the metaverse field ultimately depends on our ability to control the market in international competition. If we cannot dominate the technology path, we cannot dominate technology standards; if we cannot dominate technology standards, we cannot dominate the market; and if we cannot dominate the market, we cannot dominate governance.

The term "metaverse" is merely a symbol, representing the aggregation of the vision of the information technology revolution. When the cumulative progress in various technological fields eventually makes the metaverse a reality, it may not necessarily be called the "metaverse". Therefore, the metaverse and artificial intelligence are not concepts at the same level. With this understanding, we will not merely regard the metaverse as an investment opportunity but rather see that the metaverse concept embodies the leap that the information technology revolution will bring to human civilization.

In summary, to understand and assess the metaverse, we must look beyond appearances and grasp its essence. The metaverse is a technological and industrial high ground backed by concrete technologies, industries, applications, and demands, making it a must-win area for our country.

6.2 Working Together Toward a Metaverse Civilization

Humanity is currently in the early stages of an information civilization. The new round of technological and industrial revolutions will inevitably promote a leap in productivity, profoundly transforming production methods, social governance, and the global governance system and pushing human civilization to new heights.

Contemporary international organizations, institutions, and rules in the global governance system were primarily established by the West after World War II, needing more representation and inclusiveness and driven by hegemonic and capitalistic logic. They do not fully reflect the fundamental interests of most developing countries and the world's people. Especially with the deepening of the new round of technological and industrial revolutions and the rapid evolution of the world pattern, the contemporary global governance system urgently needs transformation. Accompanying the development of the metaverse, whether humanity can seize this opportunity to transform the global governance system and promote human civilization's development, genuinely realizing a shared human destiny, is an important issue of the era. China should and can provide a Chinese solution for humanity's transition to a more advanced stage of an information civilization.

To lead the governance of the metaverse, we must first lead its development. The metaverse is a system where physical and digital spaces intertwine, so we should promote the coordinated development of physical and digital spaces and insist on the self-control of core technologies. Infrastructure, hardware, terminals, energy, environment, and technical standards form the material foundation of the metaverse. At present, the United States "decoupling and breaking the supply chain" in the semiconductor industry has hindered China's high-tech industry development. Without high-end semiconductor manufacturing equipment, there are no high-end chips; without high-end chips, it is impossible to build the core and interactive systems of the metaverse, let alone discuss its value system. We must adhere to holistic and systematic thinking, avoid speculation and shortsightedness, and aim for buiding a modern socialist country in all respects by 2050 and an even more ambitious future, turning the metaverse into a ladder for humanity to achieve free and comprehensive development.

Endnotes

[1] Xi Jinping, *The Governance of China*, vol. 4, Beijing: Foreign Languages Press, 2022, pp. 196-197.

[2] *Encyclopedia of China*, vol. 23, Beijing: Encyclopedia of China Publishing House, 2009, p. 296.

[3] Zhang Yu and Yan Juqun, "Conceptual Analysis of 'Network Civilization'", *Qinghai Social Science*, No. 6, 2014.

[4] Xi Jinping, "Speech at the Symposium on Cybersecurity and Informatization," Beijing: People's Publishing House, 2016, p. 2.

[5] *The Collected Works of Marx and Engels*, vol. 1, Beijing: People's Publishing House, 2009, p. 602.

[6] Zhang Yu and Yan Juqun, "Discerning the Concept of 'Network Civilization'", *Qinghai Social Science*, No. 6, 2014.

[7] The term "shuttle" refers to the ability for people to access and exit the metaverse at any time and place, essentially enabling

seamless switching between physical space and digital space. When the interaction system can support this seamless transition between the real and digital worlds, it means that the integration of the "human-machine-object" has been achieved, and the metaverse reaches a developed level.

[8] Marshall McLuhan, *Understanding Media—The Extension of Man*, translated by He Daokuan, Beijing: The Commercial Press, 2000, p. 33.

[9] General Secretary Xi Jinping emphasized in his video congratulatory message to the 2021 Zhongguancun Forum on September 24, 2021, "We should jointly explore ways and methods to solve important global issues through technological innovation, jointly respond to the challenges of the times, and jointly promote the noble cause of human peace and development."

[10] Xi Jinping, *The Governance of China*, vol. 2, Beijing: Foreign Languages Press, 2017, p. 62.

[11] L. Bertalanffy, *General Systems Theory: Foundations-Development-Application*, translated by Qiu Tong and Yuan Jiaxin, Beijing: Social Science Literature Press, 1987, p. 46.

[12] Qian Xuesen and Song Jian, *Engineering Control Theory*,

vol. 1, Beijing: Science Press, 2011, p. x.

[13] H. Harken, *Information and Self-Organization: A Macroscopic Approach to Complex Systems*, translated by Guo Zhian, Chengdu: Sichuan Education Press, 1988, p. 29.

[14] Duan Xiaojun, Lin Yi, and Zhao Chengli, *Tutorial of System Science*, Beijing: Science Press, 2019, pp. 121-122; Wu Guolin(ed.), *Introduction to Natural Dialectics*, Beijing: Tsinghua University Press, 2018, pp. 39-40.

[15] Ilya Prigogine, "Time, Structure and Fluctuations," *Science*, 1978, vol. 201, no. 4358, pp. 777-785.

[16] *The Complete Works of Marx and Engels*, vol. 25, Beijing: People's Publishing House, 2001, p. 592.

[17] Zou Caineng, Zhao Qun, Zhang Guosheng, et al. "Energy Revolution: from Fossil Energy to New Energy," *Natural Gas Industry*, vol. 1, 2016.

[18] Zou Caineng, He Dongbo, Jia Chengye, et al. "The Connotation and Path of World Energy Transition and Its Significance for Carbon Neutrality," *Journal of Petroleum*, no. 2, vol. 2021.

[19] Wang Yichen, "Can the Metaverse Pass the 'Energy

Barrier'," *Economic Daily*, January 27, 2022, p. 6.

[20] Claude Elwood Shannon, "A Mathematical Theory of Communication," *The Bell System Technical Journal*, vol.27, no.3, 1948, pp. 379-423.

[21] Wu Jun, *A General History of Global Science and Technology*, Beijing: CITIC Press, 2019, p. 363.

[22] *The Collected Works of Marx and Engels*, vol. 2, Beijing: People's Publishing House, 2009, p. 14.

[23] Jeremy Rifkin, *The Empathic Civilization: The Race to Global Consciousness in a World in Crisis*, Penguin, 2009

[24] *The Collected Works of Marx and Engels*, vol. 10, Beijing: People's Publishing House, 2009, p. 668.

[25] *The Complete Works of Marx and Engels*, vol. 37, Beijing: People's Publishing House, 2019, p. 203.

[26] Sun Bolin, "Industrial Metaverse—a Bridge between the Real World and Virtual World Interoperability," *Computer Simulation*, 2022, no. 7.

[27] *The Complete Works of Marx and Engels*, vol. 31, Beijing: People's Publishing House, 1998, p. 93.

[28] Yan, Tongzhu, "Industrial Metaverse Is the Next All-True

Industrial Internet," *China Economic and Trade Journal*, 2022, no. 6.

[29] Liu Datong, Guo Kai, Wang Benkuan, et al. "A Review and Prospects of Digital Twin Technology," *Journal of Instrumentation*, vol. 11, 2018. Enis Karaarslan & Mohammed Babiker, "Digital Twin Security Threats and Countermeasures: An Introduction," 2021 International Conference on Information Security and Cryptology (ISCTURKEY), IEEE, 2021.

[30] Ren Xiaoxu, Tan Jingchao, Deng Hui, et al. "Arithmetic Network Architecture Based on End-edge Cloud Hyper-Convergence," *Computer Applications*, 2022, no. S1. Lü Tingjie and Liu Feng Liu: "Research on the Arithmetic Network in the Context of the Digital Economy," *Journal of Beijing Jiaotong University (Social Science Edition)*, 2021, no. 1.

[31] Gao Qiqi, "Sovereign Blockchain and Global Blockchain Research," *World Economy and Politics*, no. 10, 2020.

[32] Si Xiao, "Blockchain Digital Asset Property Rights Theory," *Exploration and Controversy*, no. 12, 2021.

[33] Yuan, Yuan and Yang Yongzhong, "Towards Metaverse: The Mechanism and Logic of a New Kind of the Digital Economy," *Journal of Shenzhen University (Humanities and Social Sciences*

Edition), 2022, no. 1.

[34] Zhao Xing, Qiao Lili, and Ye Ying, "A Review of Metaverse Research and Applications," *Journal of Information Resource Management*, vol. 4, 2022.

[35] *Marx and Engels Collected Works*, vol. 5, Beijing: People's Publishing House, 2009, p. 429. Marx's theory is based on the mechanical science of the 19th century. Modern machinery is generally divided into power systems, transmission systems, execution systems, and control systems, the first three of which correspond to Marx's "engine, transmission mechanism, and tool machine or work machine." In modern mechanical science, the tool machine generally refers to machine tools. This is a clarification.

[36] *The Collected Works of Marx and Engels*, vol. 5, Beijing: People's Publishing House, 2009, p. 431.

[37] *The Collected Works of Marx and Engels*, vol. 5, Beijing: People's Publishing House, 2009, pp. 432-434.

[38] *The Collected Works of Marx and Engels*, vol. 5, Beijing: People's Publishing House, 2009, p. 436.

[39] W.W. Rostow, *How It All Began: The Origins of the Modern Economy*, translated by Huang Qixiang and Ji Jianbo,

Beijing: The Commercial Press, 1997, p. 106.

[40] Jia Genliang, "The Third Industrial Revolution and Industrial Intelligence," *Chinese Social Sciences*, vol. 6, 2016.

[41] John D.N. Dionisio, William G. Burns III, & Richard Gilbert, "3D Virtual Worlds and the Metaverse: Current Status and Future Possibilities," *ACM Computing Surveys* (CSUR), 2013, vol.45, no.3, pp. 1-38. John Herrman & Kellen Browning, "Are We in the Metaverse Yet?" *The New York Times*, Jul 10, 2021. Barry Collins, "The Metaverse: How to Build a Massive Virtual World," *Forbes*, https://www.forbes.com/, Sep 25, 2021. Kim Jooyoung, "Advertising in the Metaverse: Research Agenda," *Journal of Interactive Advertising*, 2021, vol.21, no.3, pp. 141-144.

[42] Alexander Hamilton. "Report on the Subject of Manufactures (1791)," Frank W. Taussig, ed., *State Papers and Speeches on the Tariff*, Cambridge, MA: Harvard University, 1892, p.17.

[43] *The Collected Works of Marx and Engels*, vol. 1, Beijing: People's Publishing House, 2009, p. 501.

[44] Information Office of the State Council of the People's Republic of China, "Working Together to Build a Community

of Shared Future in Cyberspace," Chinese government website, November 7, 2022, http://www.gov.cn/zhengce/2022-11/07/content_5725117.htm.

[45] Xi Jinping, *The Governance of China*, vol. 4, Beijing: Foreign Languages Press, 2022, p. 201.

[46] Yuan Zeng, "The Theory of the Right to Mint Coins in the Metaverse Space," *Oriental Law Journal*, no. 2, 2022.

[47] *Selected Excerpts on Building a Cyber Power by Xi Jinping*, Beijing: Central Literature Publishing House, 2021, p. 163.

[48] *Selected Excerpts on Building a Cyber Power by Xi Jinping*, Beijing: Central Literature Publishing House, 2021, p. 155.

[49] Xi Jinping, *The Governance of China*, vol. 2, Beijing: Foreign Languages Press, 2017, p. 522.

[50] *Selected Excerpts on Building a Cyber Power by Xi Jinping*, Beijing: Central Literature Publishing House, 2021, p. 163.

[51] *The Collected Works of Marx and Engels*, vol. 10, Beijing: People's Publishing House, 2009, p. 372.

[52] Xi Jinping, "Upholding the Great Banner of Socialism with Chinese Characteristics and Uniting to Strive for the Comprehensive Construction of a Socialist Modernized Country—

Report at the 20th National Congress of the Communist Party of China," Beijing: People's Publishing House, 2022, p. 19.

[53] Xi Jinping, "Upholding the Great Banner of Socialism with Chinese Characteristics and Uniting to Strive for the Comprehensive Construction of a Socialist Modernized Country—Report at the 20th National Congress of the Communist Party of China," Beijing: People's Publishing House, 2022, p. 30.

[54] Xi Jinping, *The Governance of China*, vol. 3, Beijing: Foreign Languages Press, 2020, p. 74.

References

[1] Marx, Karl, and Friedrich Engels. *The Collected Works of Marx and Engels*, vol. 1. Beijing: People's Publishing House, 2009.

[2] Marx, Karl, and Friedrich Engels. *The Collected Works of Marx and Engels*, vol. 2. Beijing: People's Publishing House, 2009.

[3] Marx, Karl, and Friedrich Engels. *The Collected Works of Marx and Engels*, vol. 5. Beijing: People's Publishing House, 2009.

[4] Marx, Karl, and Friedrich Engels. *The Collected Works of Marx and Engels*, vol. 10. Beijing: People's Publishing House, 2009.

[5] Marx, Karl, and Friedrich Engels. *The Complete Works of Marx and Engels*, vol. 25. Beijing: People's Publishing House, 2001.

[6] Marx, Karl, and Friedrich Engels. *The Complete Works of Marx and Engels*, vol. 31. Beijing: People's Publishing House, 1998.

[7] Marx, Karl, and Friedrich Engels. *The Complete Works of Marx and Engels*, vol. 37. Beijing: People's Publishing House, 2019.

[8] Xi, Jinping. *The Governance of China*, vol. 2. Beijing: Foreign Languages Press, 2017.

[9] Xi, Jinping. *The Governance of China*, vol. 3. Beijing: Foreign Languages Press, 2020.

[10] Xi, Jinping. *The Governance of China*, vol. 4. Beijing: Foreign Languages Press, 2022.

[11] Xi, Jinping. "Upholding the Great Banner of Socialism with Chinese Characteristics and Uniting to Strive for the Comprehensive Construction of a Socialist Modernized Country: - Report at the 20th National Congress of the Communist Party of China." Beijing: People's Publishing House, 2022.

[12] Xi, Jinping. *Selected Excerpts on Building a Cyber Power*. Beijing: Central Literature Publishing House, 2021.

[13] Xi, Jinping. "Speech at the Cybersecurity and Informatization Work Symposium." Beijing: People's Publishing House, 2016.

[14] Information Office of the State Council of the People's

Republic of China. "Jointly Building a Community of Shared Future in Cyberspace." China Government Network, November 7, 2022. http://www.gov.cn/zhengce/2022-11/07/content_5725117.htm.

[15] *Encyclopedia of China*, vol. 23. Beijing: Encyclopedia of China Publishing House, 2009.

[16] Harken, H. *Information and Self-Organization: A Macroscopic Approach to Complex Systems*. Translated by Guo Zhi'an. Chengdu: Sichuan Education Press, 1988.

[17] Bertalanffy, L. *General Systems Theory: Foundations, Development, Application*. Translated by Qiu Tong and Yuan Jiaxin. Beijing: Social Science Literature Press, 1987.

[18] Rostow, W.W. *How It All Began: - The Origins of the Modern Economy*. Translated by Huang Qixiang and Ji Jianbo. Beijing: The Commercial Press, 1997.

[19] Duan, Xiaojun, Lin Yi, and Zhao Chengli. *Tutorial of System Science*. Beijing: Science Press, 2019.

[20] Gao, Qiqi. "Sovereign Blockchain and Global Blockchain Research." *World Economy and Politics*, vol. 10, 2020.

[21] Jia, Genliang. "The Third Industrial Revolution and Industrial Intelligence." *Chinese Social Sciences*, vol. 6, 2016.

[22] Liu, Datong, Guo Kai, Wang Benkuan, et al. "Review and Prospect of Digital Twin Technology." *Journal of Instrumentation*, vol. 11, 2018.

[23] Lü, Tingjie and Liu Feng. "Research on Arithmetic Networks in the Context of Digital Economy." *Journal of Beijing Jiaotong University (Social Science Edition)*, no. 1, 2021.

[24] McLuhan, Marshall. *Understanding Media: The Extensions of Man*. Translated by He Daokuan. Beijing: The Commercial Press, 2000.

[25] Qian, Xuesen, and Song Jian. *Engineering Control Theory*, vol. 1. Beijing: Science Press, 2011.

[26] Ren, Xiaoxu, Tan Jingchao, Deng Hui, et al. "Computing Power Network Architecture Based on Edge-Cloud Super-Convergence." *Computer Applications*, no. S1, 2022.

[27] Si, Xiao. "Blockchain Digital Asset Property Rights Theory." *Exploration and Controversy*, no. 12, 2021.

[28] Sun, Bolin. "Industrial Metaverse—a Bridge between the Real World and Virtual World Interoperability." *Computer Simulation*, no. 7, 2022.

[29] Wang, Yichen. "Can the Metaverse Pass the 'Energy

arrier'?" *Economic Daily*, January 27, 2022, p. 6.

[30] Wu, Guolin (ed.). *An Introduction to Natural Dialectics*. Beijing: Tsinghua University Press, 2018.

[31] Wu, Jun. *A General History of Global Science and Technology*. Beijing: CITIC Press, 2019.

[32] Yan, Tongzhu. "Industrial Metaverse is the Next All-True Industrial Internet." *China Economic and Trade Journal*, no. 6, 2022.

[33] Yuan, Yuan and Yang Yongzhong. "Towards a Metaverse: The Mechanism and Logic of a New Kind of Digital Economy." *Journal of Shenzhen University (Humanities and Social Sciences Edition)*, no. 1, 2022.

[34] Yuan, Zeng. "The Theory of the Right to Mint Coins in the Metaverse Space." *Oriental Law Journal*, no. 2, 2022.

[35] Zhang, Yu and Yan Juqun. "Discerning the Concept of 'Network Civilization.'" *Qinghai Social Science*, no. 6, 2014.

[36] Zhao, Xing, Qiao Lili, and Ye Ying. "A Review of Metaverse Research and Applications." *Journal of Information Resource Management*, vol. 4, 2022.

[37] Zheng, Shilin, Chen Zhihui, and Wang Xiangshu. "From

the Internet to the Metaverse: Industrial Development Opportunities, Challenges, and Policy Suggestions." *Industrial Economic Review*, no. 6, 2022.

[38] Zou, Caineng, He Dongbo, Jia Chengye, et al. "The Connotation, Path, and Significance of World Energy Transformation to Carbon Neutrality." *Petroleum Science*, no. 2, 2021.

[39] Zou, Caineng, Zhao Qun, Zhang Guosheng, et al. "Energy Revolution: From Fossil Energy to New Energy." *Natural Gas Industry*, no. 1, 2016.

[40] Hamilton, Alexander. "Report on the Subject of Manufactures (1791)." *In State Papers and Speeches on the Tariff*, edited by Frank W. Taussig, Cambridge, MA: Harvard University, 1892.

[41] Collins, Barry. "The Metaverse: How to Build a Massive Virtual World." *Forbes*, September 25, 2021. https://www.forbes.com/.

[42] Shannon, Claude Elwood. "A Mathematical Theory of Communication." *The Bell System Technical Journal*, vol. 27, no. 3, 1948.

[43] Karaarslan, Enis, and Mohammed Babiker. "Digital Twin Security Threats and Countermeasures: An Introduction." 2021 International Conference on Information Security and Cryptology (ISCTURKEY), IEEE, 2021.

[44] Prigogine, Ilya. "Time, Structure and Fluctuations." *Science*, vol. 201, no. 4358, 1978, pp. 777-785.

[45] Rifkin, Jeremy. *The Empathic Civilization: The Race to Global Consciousness in a World in Crisis*. Penguin, 2009.

[46] Dionisio, John D.N., William G. Burns III, and Richard Gilbert. "3D Virtual Worlds and the Metaverse: Current Status and Future Possibilities." *ACM Computing Surveys* (CSUR), vol. 45, no. 3, 2013, pp. 1-38.

[47] Herrman, John, and Kellen Browning. "Are We in the Metaverse Yet?" *The New York Times*, July 10, 2021.

[48] Jooyoung, Kim. "Advertising in the Metaverse: Research Agenda." *Journal of Interactive Advertising*, vol. 21, no. 3, 2021, pp. 141-144.